CAMBRIDGE IGCSE® BUSINESS STUDIES

Revision Guide

Paul Bentley

Acknowledgements

Cover photo © Reinhard Tiburzy / Shutterstock
Illustrations by QBS

Published by Letts Educational
An imprint of HarperCollins*Publishers*
The News Building
1 London Bridge Street
London
SE1 9GF

HarperCollins*Publishers*
Macken House, 39/40 Mayor Street Upper,
Dublin 1,
DO1 C9W8,
Ireland

ISBN 978-0-00-826014-9

First published 2018

10 9 8 7 6 5

British Library Cataloguing in Publication Data
A CIP record for this book is available from the British Library.

Commissioned by Gillian Bowman
Project managed by Rachel Allegro
Copyedited by Anastasia Vassilatou
Proofread by Dylan Hamilton
Cover design by Paul Oates
Typesetting by QBS
Production by Natalia Rebow and Lyndsey Rogers
Printed and bound in Great Britain by Ashford Colour Press Ltd.

Contents

Chapter 4 Operations management

Chapter 5 Financial information and decisions

Chapter 6 External influences on business activity

Introduction

This revision guide is designed to support your studies for the Cambridge IGCSE® and O Level in Business Studies. It covers all of the learning objectives in the Business Studies syllabuses, and will help you consolidate your learning in all areas of the course such as knowledge and understanding of key concepts, the ability to apply theories and techniques, analyse evidence, and evaluate arguments – all in a business context.

The guide is divided into six chapters. Each chapter covers one of the topics in the syllabuses.

The syllabuses contain a lot of subject-specific vocabulary that you need to learn. Key words are highlighted in bold in the main text and the definitions are summarised in the Glossary at the end of the book.

You will find Revision tips on many of the pages in the guide. They explain how to avoid some common errors that students make when they write answers to questions.

Revision is only successful if you do something active, rather than simply reading. You could try rewriting some of the material in a different form. For example, you could convert a paragraph of text into a series of bullet points, or change a set of bullet points into a table. Alternatively, you might use the content to create flashcards so that you can test yourself on key concepts.

There are Quick test questions at the end of each subtopic. Use these to check that you have understood and remembered the content you have just worked through. The answers to these questions are at the back of the book.

At the end of each chapter, there is a set of exam-style practice questions. These are designed to help you prepare for the theory parts of your examinations. Each question has a mark allocation, which you should use to help you decide how much to write, and how much detail to give in your answer. The questions, example answers, marks awarded and comments that appear in the book were written by the author. Note that in examinations, the way marks would be awarded to answers like these may be different.

You will find a list of the contents on pages 3 to 4. You could use this to keep track of your progress as you work through the guide – tick the box in one colour when you have first worked through a section and then in another colour when you have gone over it again and answered all of the questions correctly.

Business activity

Consumers have needs and wants. Needs are those goods or services that are essential to their survival, such as food and shelter. Wants are luxury items that people desire but that are not essential, such as sports cars or high-definition televisions.

Not all products and services are freely available; business managers do not have unlimited space to set up machinery or store **raw materials**. Consequently, sometimes consumers want to buy products that are in short supply.

Scarcity

Scarcity is said to exist when we have limited quantities of resources and unlimited wants.

Scarcity can have a number of effects:

* The scarcer a resource becomes, the more expensive it becomes.
* In extreme cases, governments may choose to **ration** the supply of these resources, limiting the quantity that any individual is allowed to buy.

Consumers and firms do not have unlimited quantities of resources such as time and money. This means that they must choose the best way to allocate these scarce resources:

* Managers may have to choose between an **advertising** campaign or investing in machinery.
* Consumers may have to choose between buying a new computer or going on holiday.

Whichever option we choose, we have to give up the other option. The option that we forego is the **opportunity cost** of the option that we select.

Specialisation

In order to make the most of scarce resources, many businesses choose to **specialise** in one particular type of activity. This tends to lead to increases in **productivity** and **efficiency**, meaning that firms can make greater profits for their owners. Firms might choose to specialise in a number of different activities. They might focus on manufacturing goods or making components for other firms. They might focus on providing services to consumers (e.g. wedding planning), businesses (e.g. waste disposal) or both (e.g. banking).

You must be able to:
* explain how business activity aims to fulfil the needs and wants of consumers
* discuss the impact of specialisation on firms and consumers
* evaluate the importance of adding value.

> **Revision tip**
>
> Think about how opportunity costs influence your decisions. What opportunity costs do you face when you spend your pocket money? Linking key concepts from the course to your own life and experiences should help you remember them.

Adding value

Businesses exist to transform raw materials into goods and services that consumers want to buy.

When businesses transform raw materials into something more useful to consumers, the finished product is worth more money. The transformation process creates **added value.**

For example, a baker combines flour, yeast and water to create bread. Each ingredient is relatively inexpensive on its own. When they are combined, they are in a form that is more useful to consumers. People are willing to spend more money on things that are more useful to them.

There are a number of ways that a business can add value:

- **Branding** – by using elements such as logos and slogans to make goods seem to be worth more.
- **Customer service** – by giving **customers** assistance, which helps them feel they are getting more value for their money.
- **Adding features** – by making a basic product do something that other similar products will not do.
- **Quality** – by producing a product that is superior, for example, either aesthetically or ergonomically.

> **Revision tip**

Be prepared to give examples of how a business that you are familiar with adds value to very basic ingredients. You might be able to find plenty of interesting examples at your favourite fast-food restaurant.

Quick test

1. Explain the meaning of the term 'scarcity'.
2. List five examples of goods and services that might be scarce. For each example, suggest a reason why it might be scarce.
3. Explain an opportunity cost that might be faced by:
   a) a business owner.
   b) a consumer.
4. Discuss one reason why business owners might choose to specialise in producing a specific type of good or service.
5. Analyse three ways in which a business might add value to raw materials.

Classification of business

The basis of business classification

Businesses can be organised into groups according to the type of activities they are involved in. There are three types of classification: primary, secondary and tertiary.

Definitions

Primary industry – businesses that extract raw materials from the ground or the sea.

Secondary industry – businesses that process raw materials so that they can be used.

Tertiary industry – businesses that provide a service to the public or to other firms.

This table shows some examples of businesses that fit into each classification:

Primary sector	Secondary sector	Tertiary sector
• farms • fisheries • coal mines	• oil refineries • bakeries • toy manufacturers	• supermarkets • cinemas • taxi firms

Reasons for the changing importance of business classification

Some developed countries, such as the UK, are said to have developed a **knowledge economy**, where large numbers of jobs, such as banking and software development, are in the tertiary sector. Government policy has encouraged the growth of these jobs because they are often well paid.

In many developing countries wages are often very low compared to those in developed countries. There will also be lower levels of education for many citizens, who then have fewer skills to offer employers. This means that businesses operating in primary industries such as agriculture and mining can employ large numbers of people at low costs, leading to higher profits.

As a country develops, people will gain more education and skills. They will be able to pursue higher-paying jobs and will seek these in the secondary and tertiary sectors. People will seek a higher standard of living and will be less interested in low-paying manual jobs in the primary sector.

You must be able to:
• outline different forms of business classification
• explain how to classify different types of business
• explain the significance of changes to the number of primary, secondary and tertiary firms in developed and developing countries.

> **Revision tip**

It is important to learn definitions thoroughly. Learning and understanding them will support you throughout your course and help you prepare for examinations.

Public and private sector business

It is possible to classify companies according to how they are owned.

Some companies are created by and owned by governments. These businesses are said to be part of the public sector. There are many reasons why a government might want to establish a **public sector business**. It might want to provide services such as healthcare, which might not be provided by the private sector at a price most people can afford. Alternatively, it might be to take over essential services that are failing in the private sector, such as banking. Sometimes a government sets up **public sector businesses** to develop firms in new industries, such as renewable energy, which might not be profitable enough to be worth the cost of investment for **private sector businesses**.

Businesses that are owned by private individuals are part of the private sector. These can include:

- small firms that are owned by one person or a group of partners
- incorporated firms that are owned by shareholders.

In a **mixed economy**, there will be a combination of both public and private sector businesses. Private sector firms will offer goods and services where they believe that they can fulfil the needs and wants of **consumers** profitably. Where a government believes that essential goods and services will be underprovided, it will provide them, for example, education.

> **Revision tip**

It is important to know how theory can be applied to your local business context. Can you give examples of public and private sector companies from your country?

Quick test

1. Write definitions of primary, secondary and tertiary industry.
2. Suggest examples of primary, secondary and tertiary sector activities that might be carried out by a large oil company such as Shell Oil Company.
3. Outline three differences between developed and developing economies.
4. Give two reasons why primary industry is becoming less important in developed economies.
5. Define the terms 'public sector' and 'private sector'.
6. Give two possible reasons why the government of your country might want to create public sector companies.

Enterprise and entrepreneurship

The characteristics of successful entrepreneurs

What are the qualities that make a successful entrepreneur? These vary from person to person, but many of the most successful entrepreneurs have some or all of the following characteristics to some degree:

- Charisma – the ability to inspire staff, customers and investors with their magnetic personality.
- Determination – the ability to pursue a goal, even if others are not supportive.
- Resilience – being able to 'bounce back' from failure.
- Creativity – using their imagination to come up with unique solutions to problems or designs for products.

Contents of a business plan

A **business plan** is a document that an entrepreneur can present to **stakeholders** in their business, such as potential investors. It provides essential details that can be used to judge how likely it is that a business idea will be successful.

A typical business plan will usually include:

- a summary of what the business does
- details of the aims and **objectives** of the business
- a **cashflow** forecast
- a forecasted **income statement**
- a marketing plan
- a staffing plan.

A business plan is a useful document for entrepreneurs. It can help them to remain focused on things that are important to the success of their business idea. It can also help them to monitor their progress – they can use the business plan to set out their goals for the starting up of their business. Over the course of the year they can refer back to the plan to see how close they are to achieving those goals.

Revision tip

Try to think about examples of entrepreneurship that you have seen on television. How do the people on programmes such as *The Apprentice* or *Dragons' Den* demonstrate the characteristics of entrepreneurship?

Revision tip

Imagine you are a bank manager. What would you want to see in a business plan before you would be willing to lend money to an entrepreneur?

How and why governments support business start-ups

How do governments provide help?

Many governments choose to provide assistance to entrepreneurs to make sure that their business ideas have a chance of becoming successful. Governments use a range of methods of support including:

- grants – a grant is a sum of money that must be used for a specific purpose, such as buying equipment, but the entrepreneur does not have to pay it back.
- loans – sometimes banks are not willing to lend money to entrepreneurs because they are concerned about losing their investment if the business fails. Governments can arrange loans that charge low rates of interest to encourage new businesses.
- advice – some entrepreneurs might need specific information about very specialised areas of doing business, such as how to export goods to other countries. Governments can help entrepreneurs speak to experts who can offer them assistance.
- training schemes – while entrepreneurs might have creative ideas and lots of resilience, they might not have specific skills, such as **cashflow** forecasting. Government training schemes can help provide guidance on certain aspects of running a company.

Why do governments provide help?

Reasons might include:

- reducing unemployment
- improving economic growth
- encouraging new and innovative industries to develop
- improving international competitiveness.

Quick test

1. State three characteristics of an entrepreneur.
2. Outline five things that might be included in a business plan.
3. Explain why a business plan might be essential for the success of a start-up business.
4. Discuss three ways in which a government could help entrepreneurs set up a small business.
5. Analyse two reasons why governments might want to encourage people to start new businesses.

Business growth and size

Methods of measuring business size

There are a number of ways of measuring the size of businesses, including:

- the number of people employed. When a business grows, it might need to employ more people. The European Union Statistics Agency, Eurostat, divides businesses into the following categories:

Size	Number of employees
Micro enterprise	Fewer than 10
Small enterprise	10–49
Medium enterprise	50–249
Large enterprise	250+

This classification includes not only paid employees, but also volunteers, interns and owners that work within the business.

- the value of output. The greater the financial value of the goods and/ or services that a business produces, the larger it is.
- the capital employed in the firm. This refers to the amount of money invested in the business over the long term. Larger businesses have very large amounts of investment. For example, public limited companies are likely to have significant investment from shareholders.
- market share. The size of businesses can also be measured according to how much of the market the firm serves compared to its direct competitors.

Limitations of methods of measuring business size

Different methods can produce contradictory results. A charity might have several hundred volunteers but few assets, making it large in terms of employees but small in terms of capital employed.

Why do some businesses grow and others remain small?

Why and how some businesses grow

Why do the owners of some businesses want to expand their business?

- They might want to make higher profits.
- They might want to satisfy personal goals, such as having the prestige of owning a successful company.
- They might see the opportunity to grow their business and capture market share before competitors enter the market.
- Sometimes, entrepreneurs want to add value to their business so that they can sell it on and start a new **enterprise**.

You must be able to:
- outline a range of methods of measuring the size and growth of businesses
- explain the limitations of different methods of measuring size and growth
- consider the reasons why some firms grow while others remain small.

> **Revision tip**
>
> When you are thinking about a micro enterprise, try to imagine a market stall. When you are considering large enterprises, try to imagine a supermarket chain.

There are two different types of business growth: internal and external.

Internal growth happens when a business gains new customers, increases revenue from existing customers, and/or opens new branches. This can be achieved in a number of ways: sales can be gained through successful promotional activity; more sales could be made to existing customers through clever direct marketing activity; new branches could be opened by borrowing money from banks.

External growth happens when one company buys another. There are a number of different forms of external growth:

- **Merger** – when two companies voluntarily join together into a single business.
- **Takeover** – when one business, usually a large firm, buys another business and absorbs it into its own organisation.
- **Conglomerate** – when a number of smaller firms in different markets join together to share facilities such as a marketing department.

Problems linked to business growth

When a business grows larger, this can lead to an increase in costs. These cost increases are known as **diseconomies of scale.**

Problem	Solution
Difficulty in **communication** between branches	Introduce an ICT-based communication system.
Lack of **motivation**	Create a new system of incentives to encourage workers to be more productive.
Problems in co-ordinating business activity	Redesign the organisational structure to ensure clear leadership in each part of the business.

Why some businesses remain small

Not all entrepreneurs want their business to grow. Possible reasons for this include:

- satisfaction of personal objectives. There is a trade-off between potential increased profits and the increased stress they might experience.
- a lack of resources. The necessary land, capital or labour might not be available.
- pressure from competitors. Other firms might have already gained a dominant position in the market, making growth uneconomical.

Business failure

There is a range of reasons why businesses fail. Some relate to internal factors such as poor management. Other factors are beyond the control of the owners and managers of a firm, such as a **recession**.

Internal causes of failure include:

- a lack of management skills. Not all managers are good at their jobs. Some might not be able to judge levels of demand correctly and order too much stock, causing liquidity problems. Other managers might order too little stock, causing customer dissatisfaction. Managers might struggle to ensure that staff deliver **customer service** that is consistent and reliable. This could potentially lead to negative word of mouth and ultimately deter potential customers from using that business.
- liquidity problems. **Liquidity** refers to the ability of a business to pay its bills. Money that is available to spend immediately is known as liquid **cash**. If a business invests too much money in stock and machinery, it replaces cash with illiquid assets. As long as the business has access to credit such as **overdrafts** for emergencies, this is not a problem. However, if a business runs out of cash, it could become insolvent, meaning that it does not have enough money to pay its debts. This would cause the business to fail.

External causes of failure have to do with the business environment. There are a number of ways this can change, leading to some businesses failing:

- Economic activity can slow down, leading to less **consumer spending** and therefore reducing revenues.
- Customer tastes and preferences can change, leading to fewer customers using certain businesses.
- Laws can change, leading to certain business costs rising so that some businesses are no longer profitable.

Why are new businesses at greater risk of failing?

New firms might not yet have the customer base that they need to survive. They are unlikely to have built up any reserves of retained profit to see themselves through hard times. A business with no track record of success and of paying bills on time might be seen as less creditworthy by banks, so it is less likely to be able to borrow money in an emergency.

Quick test

1. List three ways in which businesses can grow.
2. Explain the difference between internal and external growth.
3. List three reasons why businesses fail.
4. Explain why new businesses are more likely to fail.

Business organisations

Sole traders

A **sole trader** is a business that has only one owner. This type of business is normally relatively small. A sole trader is able to make all of the decisions about the running of the business themselves and does not have to share their profits with anyone else.

A sole trader is considered to be a self-employed person who does not have a separate legal identity from that of their business. This means that if someone chooses to sue the business, they are suing the owner personally.

If a sole trader's business fails, the owner can sometimes lose their personal possessions. This is because they have **unlimited liability**, which means that **trade payables** can claim money back from the owner personally if business assets are insufficient to settle debts.

Partnerships

A **partnership** is when two or more people own a business. Many partnership businesses are relatively small, but some partnerships can be large, for example:

- law firms
- accountancy practices
- the John Lewis chain of department stores in the UK.

In a partnership, decision-making is shared between the owners of the business. This will depend on the details contained in a **deed of partnership**, which will set out the specific roles and **responsibilities** of each partner. Profits are shared between the partners. The amount of profit that each partner earns will depend on their own particular role and responsibilities within the business.

Like sole traders, partnerships have unlimited liability: the personal possessions of partners can be at risk if the business fails. Liability for debts is also shared between partners. If one partner creates a debt in the name of the business, all of the other partners are responsible for that debt.

Business organisations

Limited companies

A **limited company** is owned by shareholders. Each shareholder is entitled to a share of the profits of the business in the form of a dividend. These firms benefit from **limited liability**, which means that the shareholders will lose only the money that they have invested in the business if it fails.

> **You must be able to:**
> - outline the different forms of business ownership
> - explain the advantages and disadvantages of different forms of ownership
> - justify recommendations for an appropriate form of ownership in a given situation.

> **Revision tip**
>
> A common mistake is to assume that a sole trader cannot employ staff. However, while there is only one business owner, the business can employ as many staff as it needs.

> **Revision tip**
>
> Remember that sole traders and partnerships are called unincorporated businesses.

There are two different types of limited company:

- Private Limited Company (LTD). Shares in this type of companies can only be bought and sold with the agreement of other shareholders. This type of ownership is often favoured by family businesses. These companies must submit a copy of their accounts to the government each year. This information can be accessed by the public if they request it.
- Public Limited Company (PLC). Shares in this type of company can be sold on the stock market. Anyone over the age of 18 can purchase shares in the company. Shareholders must be informed of the performance of the business, and if profits are going to be lower than expected, the information must be shared with shareholders. If shareholders are unhappy with the management of a PLC, they can vote on the reappointment of directors at the **annual general meeting**. A PLC must publish an annual report each year giving details of its performance, such as accounts.

Franchises

A **franchise** is an agreement between an existing business with a successful brand and an individual or a small firm. The agreement allows the smaller firm to set up branches of the established and popular business. An example of a business that uses franchising is McDonald's. Many of McDonald's restaurants are not owned by McDonald's, but by other companies that have paid an annual fee for the right to trade under the McDonald's name.

> **Revision tip**
>
> Franchise is not a form of business ownership; it is a business model. Franchises can be owned by sole traders, partnerships or limited companies.

Joint ventures

This is when two companies work together to set up a new firm or a new brand. This might be done to allow the sharing of costs or expertise between the firms. An example of a **joint venture** is the delivery firm UPS, which recently set up a company with a Chinese firm called SF Holdings to transport packages, initially from the USA to China.

Differences between types of business organisation

Sole traders and **partnerships** are known as **unincorporated businesses**; they have no legal identity that is separate from that of their owners. If someone takes legal action against one of these firms, they are taking legal action against the owners. In contrast, limited companies have a legal identity that is separate from that of their owners.

Risk

Different types of business ownership have different levels of risk. Unincorporated businesses have higher levels of risk for their owners because:

- the owner has unlimited liability
- the owner has no separate legal identify from that of the business
- the owner is likely to have invested a higher portion of their personal wealth into setting up the business than might be the case with someone buying shares in a **limited company**.

Choosing a suitable form of business ownership

The most suitable form of business ownership depends on a number of factors:

- What are the goals of the entrepreneur?
- What entrepreneurial characteristics do they possess?
- How quickly do they want the business to grow?
- What type of business are they planning to set up?
- What are the current market conditions?

Public sector businesses

A public sector business is one that is owned by the government of a country. Sometimes this is because such businesses are of vital national interest, for example, nuclear power stations and transport **infrastructure**, and sometimes this is because they operate in sectors that might not survive commercially but are considered to be important to long-term economic performance, for example, renewable energy.

The number of companies that are part of the public sector will depend on the type of government in a particular country. Some governments, for example in France, believe in maintaining nationalised industries to protect workers and national interests. Governments in other countries, for example the UK, prefer to leave as many companies as possible in private ownership. They want to avoid having too much state ownership, which they believe is bad for **enterprise**.

Quick test

1. State three benefits of being a sole trader.
2. State three drawbacks of being in a partnership.
3. Explain the meaning of the term 'unincorporated business'.
4. Discuss the benefits to a sole trader of becoming a limited company.
5. Explain why owners of unincorporated businesses face higher levels of risk.
6. List three things that you should consider when choosing a form of business ownership.
7. Explain two differences between a public sector and a private sector firm.

Business and stakeholder objectives

Business objectives

The owners and managers of a business need to know what they plan to achieve and how they are going to go about this. Having a clear idea about the direction of a company becomes increasingly important as it grows because increasing numbers of staff will have to share a common understanding of where the company is going.

Most businesses will have a number of **objectives**. Objectives are the targets that a business owner hopes to achieve in a given period of time.

The objectives that businesses set will vary according to a number of factors, such as the market the firm operates in, the behaviour of competitors, the goals of the owners and the stage of the product lifecycle that a business has reached. Typical objectives might include:

- survival. A new business, one with a lot of competitors or one that is in a declining industry, might focus on simply keeping going.
- growth. Both new and existing businesses might aim for growth. This could be for a number of reasons, including:
  - to gain **economies of scale**
  - to remain **competitive** compared to new firms entering the market
  - to increase the amount of **profit** made
  - to take advantage of a new opportunity.
- profit. A business might set an objective to either make a specific amount of profit or to make a specific **profit margin** on its sales.
- market share. A business might aim to capture a specific percentage of all sales in its market.

Objectives of social enterprises

Social enterprises are businesses that exist to do good for the community or specific groups in society. They are likely to have different goals to those of **private sector businesses**. For example, they might aim:

- to raise awareness of a cause
- to support a specific number of people or groups
- to generate a financial surplus to invest in future plans.

Objectives of public sector firms

Companies owned by the government are likely to have different objectives. These might include:

- to provide public goods
- to improve economic development in poorer areas
- to provide essential **infrastructure**.

Business and stakeholder objectives

Stakeholders are groups or individuals that are affected in some way by the activities of the business. Stakeholders can be either internal or external:

- Internal stakeholders are those individuals or groups within the business.
- External stakeholders are those individuals or groups outside the business.

Different stakeholder groups are likely to have their own aims and objectives. Sometimes these differing objectives can lead to conflict. For example, the employees of a firm are likely to want higher wages, but this conflicts with the aim of business owners to make higher levels of profit.

	Stakeholders	Objectives
Internal	Employees – people who work for the business, including full- and part-time staff, temporary and permanent workers.	• to earn higher wages • better terms and conditions of work • access to better training and development
Internal	Managers – people who deal with the day-to-day running of a business on behalf of its owners.	• acknowledgement of status, for example, a company car, a better job title • opportunities for advancement • job-enrichment opportunities, for example, input into strategic decision-making
Internal	Owners – people who invested money in the business and own some or all of the equity in the business.	• to make higher profits • to minimise costs • to increase market share
External	Suppliers – firms that provide raw materials for making goods, machinery and equipment, and/or services such as telephone lines or internet connections.	• to charge the highest possible price for goods/services provided • to be awarded future contracts
External	Government – the group of politicians which leads the country, setting tax levels and deciding to what extent to regulate businesses and influence business activity.	• to reduce unemployment figures • to maximise tax revenue • to ensure the economy is competitive internationally • to maximise economic growth
External	Trade payables – firms or individuals to whom the business owes money, for example, banks and suppliers.	• to collect outstanding debts within agreed timescales • to secure new contracts to provide credit facilities in the future
External	Customers – people who make purchases from the business, buying goods or services for themselves or for others who are the final consumers.	• to pay the lowest possible prices • to receive high levels of customer service

Quick test

1. Define the term 'objective'.
2. Why do businesses set objectives?
3. List four objectives that a business might set.
4. Define the term 'stakeholder'.
5. Give three examples of external stakeholders in a business.

Exam-style practice questions

1 Broadside! is a children's soft-play business with a pirate theme. It operates on a retail park outside a major city. The business has grown rapidly with support from the government.

Broadside! serves the needs of a range of customers from poorer and more affluent parts of the city. The owner of the business operates as a sole trader and gave up a well-paid job to set up the business. The owner believes that risk-taking is the most important attribute of a successful entrepreneur.

a) Define "needs". [2]

b) Define "sole trader". [2]

c) Outline how support from the government might help Broadside! to grow. [4]

d) Explain two ways that the owner of Broadside! could measure the growth of the business. [6]

e) Do you believe that risk-taking is the most successful attribute for an entrepreneur? Justify your answer. [6]

2 Burger Kitchen

Chad owns a burger kitchen franchise in Main City in country X. Chad likes the fact that the franchisor gives him advice and support to help him run the business and he likes the promotional campaigns that are run by the head office, but he finds the lack of freedom to make decisions frustrating.

Chad runs the business as a partnership with his brother but he is considering becoming a private limited company. He thinks that this might be the best way to reduce the risks related to his main objective to increase the market share of the restaurant.

Chad has recently encountered problems with a pressure group. They sometimes demonstrate outside his restaurant in protest at the relationship between fast foods such as burgers and higher rates of obesity. Chad's staff find it stressful coming to work on days when there is a protest.

The Great Burger Company owns a farm to grow potatoes and raise cattle. They believe that this gives them more control of their supply chain. This year, however, the number of potatoes grown on their farm has been greatly reduced due to poor weather. This has led to increased costs for the business when buying potatoes. In response to this, the company is considering two options – either increasing the price of chips or buying lower quality potatoes from abroad.

a) Explain two possible reasons why Chad might want the business to become a private limited company [8]

b) Explain why the following three factors are important to Chad when running the business as a franchise:

- help and support

- centralised promotional campaigns

- freedom to make decisions

Which factor do you think is most important? Justify your answer. [12]

c) Explain two objectives that Chad might set for his Great Burger Company franchise. [8]

d) State the impact of the Great Burger Company franchise on three stakeholders:

- pressure groups

- staff

- customers

Which group is most affected by the business? Justify your answer. [12]

e) Explain why primary, secondary and tertiary industry are important to the Great Burger Company franchisees such as Chad. [8]

f) Consider the two different responses to the scarcity of potatoes that the Great Burger Company have examined:

- increasing the price of chips

- importing lower quality potatoes from abroad

Which option do you think the Great Burger Company should choose? Justify your answer. [8]

Motivating employees

The importance of a well-motivated workforce

Having a well-motivated workforce can have a significant impact on the productivity and profitability of a business. It is important for business owners and managers to understand how and why people can be motivated or demotivated.

Why people work

What is **motivation**? Motivation occurs when a person wants to do something, such as a particular work task.

The concept of human needs

Some theorists believe that people have specific needs that must be met for them to feel motivated. Maslow's hierarchy of needs is an important example of this type of theory.

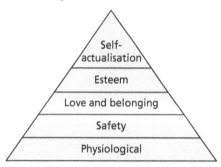

The higher a worker can move up the hierarchy, the more motivated they become. According to Maslow, workers must pass through each level in order. If the needs at one level are not met, it is not possible to move any higher up the hierarchy.

Key motivational theories

Taylor proposed a theory called scientific management. This theory suggests that all workers are lazy and will try to avoid work. In this theory, the only thing that will motivate workers to do more is money. Therefore, Taylor proposed that jobs be broken up into small tasks that can be easily measured and monitored. Each worker should be given a specific job to do. The more work they complete, the more they will be paid.

Herzberg's two-factor theory builds on Maslow's hierarchy. Human needs are split into two groups:

- **Hygiene factors** are factors such as pay, safe working conditions, relationships with others and supervision. They cannot cause motivation, but if they are absent from the workplace, they will cause demotivation.
- **Motivators** are factors such as opportunities for promotion, training and development, feedback and praise. They will cause workers to be motivated. The more relevant each factor is to a worker, the more motivated they will become.

According to Herzberg, businesses must ensure that **hygiene factors** are addressed or staff cannot be motivated. In order to motivate staff, **motivators** must be addressed to make staff want to work.

Methods of motivation

Financial rewards:

- Wage – a sum of money paid regularly to workers, usually a fixed sum of money for each hour that they work
- Salary – an annual sum of money paid in monthly instalments to the worker
- Bonus – a payment in addition to a wage or salary, usually paid for meeting individual performance targets
- Commission – a percentage of the revenue generated by the employee that is paid to them in addition to any wage or salary earned
- Profit-sharing – when a business meets goals, a proportion of its profits are shared amongst employees

Non-financial methods of motivation:

- Job enrichment – giving workers extra **responsibilities** to make their job more challenging and more interesting
- Job rotation – moving workers from one task to another systematically so that they do not have a chance to get bored
- Teamworking – fulfilling the social needs of workers by giving them a chance to work alongside other employees and giving them a sense of belonging
- Training – allowing workers to develop new skills, giving them a sense of achievement and improving their self-esteem
- Opportunities for promotion – giving workers something to focus on which may make them work harder to 'prove themselves'

Recommend and justify appropriate methods of motivation in given circumstances

The most appropriate method of motivation in any given situation might depend on a number of factors, for example:

- The type of staff that you want to motivate, for example, permanent or temporary
- What you hope to achieve by motivating your staff, for example, a temporary burst of extra work or a permanent increase in productivity
- The existing level of motivation of your staff
- The resources that you have available to motivate your staff

Quick test

1. Define the term 'motivation'.
2. List three different theories of motivation.
3. Explain the difference between financial and non-financial incentives.

Draw, interpret and understand simple organisational charts

Simple hierarchical structures

A tall organisation has a long **chain of command** because there are several layers of management and supervisory staff. A flat organisation has fewer layers of managers and supervisors, but senior staff have to look after more employees, which creates a larger **span of control**.

You must be able to:
- produce a diagram of an organisation's structure
- outline the relationship between different job roles
- explain the impact of management on a business.

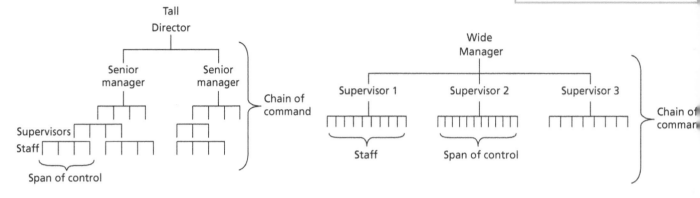

Roles and responsibilities

As people move further up the hierarchy of a business, their **job role** will change and they will gain additional **responsibilities**. Every business has its own specific job roles, but typical examples might include:

- directors. In public and private limited companies, directors run the business on behalf of the owners. They make the main strategic decisions and set goals for the company.
- managers. Managers work under the directors. Their role is to work out how best to use the available resources to achieve the company's goals.
- supervisors. Supervisors work with the managers to make sure that the business runs smoothly from day to day. Supervisors monitor the work of shop-floor staff and deal with serious or non-routine issues with customers.

Inter-relationships between job roles

Even when they are not in the same team, different members of staff will rely on each other in a number of ways. Shop-floor workers might depend on the finance department to pay bills on time so that they have the equipment they need. Managers might rely on directors to set clear targets so that they know what they are supposed to achieve.

> **Revision tip**
>
> When you are trying to remember hierarchies, think about the structure of your school. Your head teacher and their deputies are like directors, the heads of departments are like managers, and teachers are like supervisors.

The role of management

Managers run a business from day to day on behalf of its owners. The job of a manager fulfils a number of important functions. Functions of management include:

- planning. While the owners or directors of a business set the overall goals for the company, managers make plans to ensure that those goals are met.
- organising. Managers make sure that the right resources are available at the right times. This might mean organising rotas so that enough staff are available, or ensuring that there is enough machinery and equipment available to complete tasks.
- co-ordinating. Managers make sure that their resources are in the right places at the right time. This might mean making sure that staff have staggered breaks, or making sure that machinery is set up, or that raw materials are brought out of storage for a particular time.
- commanding. Managers give directions that must be followed to junior employees.
- controlling. Managers are in overall charge of the activities that take place from day to day and make sure that tasks are completed so that goals can be achieved.

Importance of delegation

Delegation is when a manager (or other senior employee) gives a colleague the authority for completing a task. However, the responsibility for completing that task remains the manager's: if the person delegated to do the job does it badly or even if they fail to do it, the manager will still have to answer for the result.

Trust versus control

Managers who delegate tasks have to trust their staff – they need to have faith that they will complete these tasks. But managers who delegate tasks also have less control over how they are done. An employee might have a different way of doing something, or might have different ideas about the standards that have to be achieved. Unfortunately, the only way managers can completely control how a piece of work is done is to do it themselves. This would take up too much of their time, which is why some jobs have to be delegated.

Quick test

1. Draw a hierarchy diagram for an organisation that you have learned about on your course.
2. Explain the differences between 'chain of command' and 'span of control'.
3. Explain why managers are important to the success of a business.

Leadership styles

Features of the main leadership styles

- **Autocratic**
  This type of leader issues orders to workers and expects them to be followed. They believe that their view is best and that there is no need to consider the opinions of staff.
- **Democratic**
  This type of leader involves workers in decision-making processes. They take account of the views and preferences of workers when they set goals. Once goals have been agreed, they will monitor and control the work that is completed to ensure that goals are achieved.
- **Laissez-faire**
  This type of leader lets workers approach tasks in their own way. They do not give them instructions on how to work but may support and encourage them. They do not monitor the work completed by employees and they let staff set their own goals and targets.

Recommend and justify an appropriate leadership style in given circumstances

Is there a correct type of leadership? Not necessarily. The best type of leadership is likely to depend on circumstances.

- During a crisis, an **autocratic** leader might be able to get things done quickly and make sure that things get done when they need to be done.
- When a firm has a lot of skilled workers and plenty of time to make decisions, it might be best to take a **democratic** approach so that the business can benefit from the expertise of all its staff.
- A firm with a lot of highly skilled and well-educated workers might benefit from a **laissez-faire** approach from time to time. For example, Google have seen many valuable products come from the 'G Time' that they give staff to work on their own ideas.

Trade unions

What is a trade union?

A **trade union** is an organisation that represents the interests of workers. It will negotiate deals on wages and working conditions with managers on behalf of its members. This process is called **collective bargaining**.

When workers feel they are being exploited or otherwise treated unfairly, unions can organise **industrial action** on behalf of their members. This can take many forms:

- Strikes – when employees refuse to work for a period of time. This might be for a set number of days or it might be for an indefinite amount of time.
- Work to rule – when workers fulfil their contractual obligations but do nothing else. For example, they might not help in other departments or do any overtime.

You must be able to:
- outline different leadership styles
- justify a recommendation for an appropriate leadership style in a given situation
- explain the purpose of trade unions in a business.

 Revision tip

When you think of autocratic leaders, try to think of a stern military leader shouting commands at their troops.

 Revision tip

Try to think of democratic leaders as being like politicians inviting people to vote on their ideas.

Unions can also provide a number of services for workers:

- Representation during disciplinary meetings
- Special deals on insurance and other financial services
- Opportunities for education and training

The effects of employees being union members

When employees are members of a union, this can have a number of different effects:

- Less time might be spent on negotiating deals for wages. This is because the firm only has to agree a deal with the union rather than with individual workers.
- The union might use the threat of **industrial action** to force firms to pay workers higher wages.

Quick test

1. Outline two different types of leadership.
2. Recommend an appropriate form of leadership for a business that is in danger of becoming bankrupt. Give a reason for your answer.
3. Define the term 'trade union'.
4. Discuss the benefits of being in a trade union for employees.

Recruitment and selection methods

What is the difference between internal recruitment and external recruitment?

Internal recruitment is when a person that already works for a business is appointed to a new position. This might be a promotion or it might be a lateral move. Sometimes, part-time employees might be appointed to a full-time job.

External recruitment is when a person that does not currently work for a company is appointed to a job.

	Advantages	Disadvantages
Internal recruitment	• The staff member is already known and they know how the business works. • It is cheaper than external recruitment, for example, there is no cost of advertising the vacancy. • The strengths and weaknesses of the staff member are known to their manager.	• Recruitment will be from a limited pool of potential candidates. • The member of staff who is promoted or moved may still need to be replaced.
External recruitment	• It introduces new ideas from outside the business. • The number of potential applicants is larger.	• It is more expensive than internal recruitment. • It takes longer than internal recruitment.

You must be able to:
• outline the benefits and drawbacks of different forms of recruitment
• explain the process of recruiting a new member of staff
• justify a recommendation for the most appropriate potential employee in a given situation.

Revision tip

Try to connect the concept of internal and external recruitment to events in your school. Have any of your teachers been promoted to lead a department? This is an example of internal recruitment.

What are the main stages in the recruitment and selection of employees?

The following are the stages in the recruitment and selection of employees:

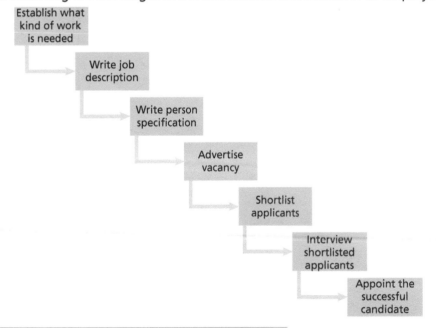

Recommend and justify who to employ in given circumstances

Deciding who to hire should normally be a case of picking someone that is the best match to the **person specification**. But what if there are other circumstances to take into consideration? A business that has a lot of new or trainee workers might prefer to hire someone with a lot of experience. Some businesses like to hire workers that have a physical appearance that matches their **brand image**. Ultimately, it is up to the owners and managers of a business who they hire as long as they do not break any **discrimination** legislation.

Benefits and limitations of part-time employees and full-time employees

There is no universally accepted definition of full- and part-time workers. This tends to vary from employer to employer. Sometimes, a part-time worker can be **flexible** and will occasionally work as many hours as a full-time employee, but not always.

	Benefits	Limitations
Full-time	• Staff are committed to working a full week. • They will develop more skills and gain more experience than part-time staff while doing more hours of work.	• Staff cost more than part-time workers. • There is less scope for flexibility with their hours than for part-time staff.
Part-time	• Staff might have more scope for working flexibly. • They have lower wage costs than full-time staff.	• It might be more challenging to communicate with part-time staff. • Part-time staff may have less experience than full-time workers.

Quick test

1. Outline the stages in recruiting a new member of staff.
2. Explain the benefits of using internal recruitment to hire a new manager.
3. Discuss the benefits of hiring full-time workers.

The importance of training and the methods of training

Importance of training to a business and employees

Training is when workers are given the opportunity to develop new knowledge and skills, and improve their existing knowledge and skills. This is important because it enables workers to perform their jobs more efficiently, and it can also lead to improvements in their **motivation**.

Benefits and limitations of induction training, on-the-job training and off-the-job training

Induction training is delivered to new workers when they first start their employment. It covers a combination of basic skills that they need to do the job as well as company procedures relating to practical matters such as booking annual leave.

On-the-job training is when an employee receives training in their place of work, often at their workstation.

Off-the-job training is when an employee receives training at a location away from their place of work, for example, a local college or the company's head office.

	Benefits	Limitations
Induction training	• Staff will become familiar with their workplace and will have few (or no) anxieties about carrying out basic tasks.	• It covers only basic tasks and knowledge so does not greatly improve workers' productivity.
On-the-job training	• It is cheaper than off-the-job training. • It is related to the specific tasks that an employee will carry out at work. • It enables employees to build good working relationships with their colleagues.	• Employees might teach bad working habits to each other. • It does not bring new ideas into the business.
Off-the-job training	• Employees may bring new ideas back to the workplace. • It gives workers time away from their daily tasks to focus on learning new skills.	• It is more expensive than on-the-job training. • It might not relate specifically to the tasks being carried out in the workplace.

Revision tip

Try to find case study examples of the effectiveness of the different types of training. Then practise applying your knowledge to the case study examples.

Why reducing the size of the workforce might be necessary

The difference between dismissal and redundancy

- **Dismissal** is when an employee has failed to work to an adequate standard. This might be because of a lack of **capability** or it might be a result of their **conduct**. For example, an employee might be dismissed for:
  - stealing company property
  - failing to improve the quality of their work after being given opportunities to do so.
- **Redundancy** is when a worker does a job that is no longer needed. For example, self-service checkouts in supermarkets mean that these companies need fewer people to operate tills. Therefore, some of the workers doing these jobs will become redundant. When a business chooses to downsize, it often offers workers the opportunity to take **voluntary redundancy**.

Understand situations in which downsizing the workforce might be necessary

- **Automation**
  When technology replaces jobs, fewer manual workers are needed. For example, computer-aided manufacturing means fewer staff are needed to operate machines such as lathes.
- Reduced **demand** for products
  Sometimes a business downsizes because it is not very successful, or its products have reached the end of their lifecycle. For example, Kodak stopped making film for cameras when the growth of digital photography made this unprofitable.

Recommend and justify which employees to make redundant in given circumstances

Knowing which workers to make redundant in any given situation can be challenging. Some firms operate a "last in, first out" policy, which means that those workers that have most recently been hired are made redundant first.

When selecting which staff to make redundant, business owners will need to consider the skills that they will need in the future. If possible, they should try to make staff who have skills that are no longer relevant redundant.

Quick test

1. Name the different forms of training.
2. Explain why training is important.
3. Give two reasons why a business might reduce the size of its workforce.
4. Discuss the potential impact of downsizing on:
   a) the firm.
   b) employees.

Legal controls over employment issues and their impact on employers and employees

Legal controls over employment contracts

Different countries have different rules about the terms that must be included in a **contract**. For example, in Europe there is a limit on the number of hours that can be worked per week.

Unfair dismissal

Most employment law is based on the principle that workers must be treated reasonably. This is especially important when making decisions to dismiss workers. When a worker is dismissed after a disciplinary process that is unreasonable, the worker may have been unfairly dismissed. If a worker is unfairly dismissed, they may be able to take the business to an **employment tribunal** to get their job back or receive compensation.

Discrimination

Most countries have laws that prohibit discrimination against people on grounds such as:

- disability
- gender
- sexuality
- race
- religion.

This can apply both to employment practices, such as who is hired or how workers are treated, but it can also apply to customers. For example, hotels are not allowed to refuse to give customers a room on the grounds of their sexuality.

Health and safety

Businesses must ensure that they have a workplace that is safe for staff and customers. Machinery must have appropriate safety equipment installed, and workers handling chemicals must have protective equipment such as gloves and goggles.

Legal minimum wage

A minimum wage is when governments pass a law that guarantees workers a certain amount of money per hour in wages. This must be paid by their employers. This reduces poverty among workers in low-skill jobs. However, it also increases employment costs and reduces the number of workers that firms are willing to hire.

> ### You must be able to:
> - outline a range of legal issues that affect the employment of staff
> - explain the impact of different legal factors on a range of companies.

> ### Revision tip
>
> Look in newspapers for examples of people who have been discriminated against at work. These examples will help you learn this topic and also help you prepare for your examinations.

Quick test

1. List five types of law that might affect businesses.
2. Explain one way in which a law might affect the recruitment of a worker.
3. Explain one way in which a law might affect the production of goods.

Why effective communication is important and the methods used to achieve it

Effective communication and its importance to business

Effective **communication** matters to businesses for a number of reasons. It is important to communicate effectively with **consumers** so they have appropriate expectations of the service that they will receive.

It is important to communicate effectively with staff so they understand their **job roles** and have the information that they need to work effectively.

It is important to communicate effectively with the owners of a business so they understand the strategies being pursued by managers and how these will affect their investment.

Benefits and limitations of different communication methods, including those based on information and communications technology (ICT)

Method of communication	Benefits	Limitations
Face-to-face conversations	• Participants can observe each other's body language.	• There may not be an accurate record of the conversation.
Telephone conversations	• They allow instant communication even when employees are in different locations.	• They do not allow participants to observe each other's body language.
Meetings	• They enable communication amongst groups of people.	• They can be time-consuming. • Employees with strong personalities can dominate discussions.
Staff noticeboards	• They are a low-cost method of communication. • They can allow communication with large numbers of people.	• Staff might not see everything that is posted. • They can be ignored.

> **Revision tip**
>
> Look for examples of effective communication at your school. What kind of messages are placed on noticeboards? What kind of messages are communicated using letters? Why are meetings sometimes used instead of notices or letters?

Method of communication	Benefits	Limitations
Emails	• They create a record of messages and responses. • They allow instant **communication**.	• They are not secure unless they are encrypted. • Employees might use emails for personal messages, wasting the company's time.
Video conferencing	• Enables employees from different countries to communicate.	• Depends on good internet connections.

Recommend and justify which communication method to use in given circumstances

The most appropriate method of communication to use will depend on a number of issues, such as:

- how quickly the message needs to be shared
- whether a written copy of the message is needed
- whether the communication needs to be one-way or two-way.

Demonstrate an awareness of communication barriers

How communication barriers arise

A **communication barrier** is when something prevents messages being shared in an accurate and timely fashion.

Problems of ineffective communication

When communication is ineffective, this can cause a number of problems. Resources might not be available in the locations or quantities required. Staff might perform tasks to a poor standard or may not complete tasks at all.

How communication barriers can be reduced or removed

Removing barriers to communication depends on the type of barrier:

- Physical barriers to communication can be removed by reorganising office space to provide clear spaces for people to talk, unobstructed by walls or furniture.
- Environmental barriers to communication can be removed by providing appropriate spaces for communication.
- Cultural barriers to communication can be overcome by providing training and advice to staff to modify their behaviour.

Quick test

1. Outline two reasons why effective communication is important to businesses.
2. Describe three methods of communication.
3. Explain how two barriers to communication could be overcome.
4. Explain the consequences of poor communication.

Exam-style practice questions

1 Fresh Sounds is a record shop which sells vinyl records and second-hand CDs. It has one branch in a small city in country B. The business employs eight members of staff. The staff are poorly motivated and often spend time when they should be working looking at mobile phones and browsing the internet.

Workers complain that no financial motivators other than a wage are provided, and that no non-financial motivators are provided at all. The owner of the shop recently appointed a new manager to deal with these problems. The new manager of the store said: "I think that the problem with these staff is that they have not been properly managed before. No one has taken action to motivate them, nor have they tried to stop them becoming demotivated."

a) Define 'motivation'. **[2]**

b) Define 'non-financial motivation'. **[2]**

c) Outline how the span of control for the manager at Fresh Sounds might impact on the motivation of workers. **[4]**

d) Explain two factors, using Maslow's hierarchy of needs, that the manager of Fresh Sounds should consider when trying to motivate staff. **[6]**

e) Do you think that motivating workers is the most important function of a manager? Justify your answer. **[6]**

2 WeCan is a manufacturing business which produces tinned goods such as baked beans and peas for supermarkets in country B. The business has been owned by the same family for 50 years and the current managing director takes an autocratic approach to leading staff. His word is final and he takes no arguments. He has refused to allow staff to join a trade union and prefers to negotiate wages with staff individually based on their performance. He feels that collective bargaining rewards lazy workers. He believes that the protection trade unions provide to workers makes it too difficult to discipline underperforming staff. He is concerned that unions might create bad relationships with workers, which could lead to industrial action.

The business has been very busy during a recent recession as more people have relied on tinned food. Several supervisor job vacancies have been created. The managing director plans to fill these vacancies using internal recruitment. Rather than drawing up person specifications for the vacancies, the managing director has simply hired staff based on his own opinion of the skills that they have.

WeCan also owns a small wholesale company, focusing on upmarket products. This company has struggled in recent years due to a lack of demand, and, as a result, the managing director has decided to downsize operations to cut costs. The main method of achieving these cuts in costs will be to make staff redundant. The managing director has decided to review the work done by staff and will use this information to make compulsory redundancies.

a) Explain two possible benefits of autocratic leadership. **[8]**

b) Explain why the following three trade union activities might be beneficial to workers:

- collective bargaining

- protection of rights

- industrial action

Which activity is most important? Justify your answer. [12]

c) Explain two possible benefits of using internal recruitment for the supervisor vacancies. [8]

d) Explain four possible implications of downsizing the WeCan wholesale business. [8]

e) Consider the decision by the managing director to make staff redundant. He has two choices:

- select the workers to be made redundant himself.

- ask for volunteers from the workforce who are willing to accept redundancy.

Which option should the managing director choose? Justify your answer. [12]

Marketing, competition and the consumer

Identifying customer needs

The purpose of marketing is to identify and satisfy **customer needs** at a profit. If a business does not understand the needs of potential customers, it will be unable to satisfy them.

Businesses use different types of market research to identify and understand the needs of their customers.

Satisfying customer needs

When a business understands its customers' needs, it is able to provide goods and services that will meet or exceed those needs. If this satisfies customers, they are more likely to return to use the business again in the future.

Maintaining customer loyalty

It is cheaper for a business to retain its existing customers than it is to attract new customers; therefore, it is important to maintain **customer loyalty**. Some businesses use loyalty schemes to maintain customer loyalty. For example, **retailers** use loyalty cards that give customers points when they make a purchase.

Building customer relationships

Many businesses use data from loyalty cards to build **customer relationships**. By looking at previous purchases, they are able to understand the type of products that customers want, and to give them special offers that are more relevant to their needs.

Concepts of mass marketing and niche marketing

There are two different types of markets that businesses can target: mass and **niche markets**.

Mass markets

This is when a business produces a product that is designed to meet the needs of the majority of the customers in a market. Products are normally made in large quantities so that the business can benefit from **economies of scale**. This is important because there are likely to be a number of businesses in a **mass market**. This means that it is likely that there will be heavy price **competition** and consequently lower revenue from each sale.

Niche markets

This is when products or services are designed to satisfy the needs of a specific group of **consumers** in the market. These goods or services are likely to be produced in smaller quantities, and will appeal to a relatively small number of potential customers. Lower quantities of **production** mean that businesses will not be able to gain economies of scale and therefore must charge higher prices.

> **You must be able to:**
> - outline the importance of meeting customer needs
> - explain the differences between mass and niche markets
> - consider the implications of targeting mass and niche markets for a range of firms.

> **Revision tip**
>
> Consider your needs when buying a range of products. What makes you buy different goods? How do the goods you buy satisfy your needs?

Benefits and limitations of both approaches to marketing

	Benefits	Limitations
Mass markets	• Large number of potential customers • Ability to mass-produce goods and gain economies of scale	• Large number of competitors • Likely to charge competitive prices, leading to lower profit margins
Niche markets	• Potential to charge high prices • Precisely match the needs of customers • Less **competition** than mass markets	• Lower number of potential customers • Goods are likely to be made using **batch production**, meaning there is less potential for economies of scale

Quick test

1. Why is it important to meet customer needs?
2. What is the meaning of the term 'customer loyalty'?
3. Why is it important for firms to build relationships with customers?
4. What is the difference between a mass market and a niche market?

Markets are dynamic. Patterns of **consumer** behaviour change over time in response to a range of different factors.

Why customer/consumer spending patterns may change

- Fashions – if a product becomes popular, customers may suddenly spend a lot of money on it, for example, fidget spinners. These trends can end just as quickly as they begin.
- Economic changes – if the **economy** goes into a **recession**, customers may stop buying premium-price goods and start shopping at discount stores more regularly.
- Changes in technology – New technologies not only enable the creation of new products and services, they also allow complementary goods and services to be developed. For example, improvements in broadband internet connections mean that more people are taking out subscriptions to video-on-demand services such as Netflix.

The importance of changing customer needs

If a business is not able to continue producing goods and services that meet **customer needs**, it is likely to suffer declines in revenue as it loses customers to other firms that can better meet their needs.

Why some markets have become more competitive

Changes in the lifestyles of consumers' tastes and preferences have meant that some **niche markets** have grown in size, attracting more firms. Improvements in technology, such as print-on-demand technology for books, have also led to opportunities for larger firms such as Amazon to enter markets that might previously have been too small for them to consider.

How businesses can respond to changing spending patterns and increased competition

The reactions of businesses vary according to the strategy of each firm and the resources available to it. Large technology companies such as Microsoft and Google often buy smaller companies that have developed innovative technologies in new and emerging markets.

Other companies might invest in research and development to produce their own responses to new developments in markets.

How and why market segmentation is undertaken

Market segmentation is the division of a market into smaller groups of customers so that businesses can use their resources more efficiently by targeting specific groups of people that are more likely to purchase their goods and services.

You must be able to:
- explain why markets change.
- explain the ways in which firms can respond to changes in markets
- justify statements about the importance of segmenting markets.

> **Revision tip**
>
> Can you think of any of your needs that have changed in the last five years? How many of those changes were due to changes in technology?

Markets can be segmented according to:

- age. For example, in the market for holidays, companies might target younger people with beach holidays near nightclubs and bars. It might target pensioners with holidays in locations that are easily accessible.
- socio-economic grouping. For example, more **affluent consumers** might be targeted for sophisticated premium-price goods.
- location. People have different types of needs in different parts of the world. People who live in warmer countries have different clothing needs from those customers in colder climates.
- gender. Men and women might be interested in different products. For example, manufacturers of cosmetics make different deodorants for men and women.

Potential benefits of segmentation to businesses

- A business is able to gain a greater market share by targeting people who are interested in its products.
- It can make more efficient use of its resources by targeting adverts at groups who are likely to be receptive to them.
- Its marketing messages can be tailored to the needs of the group being targeted, making them more relevant to its audience.

Recommend and justify an appropriate method of segmentation in given circumstances

The correct method of **market segmentation** will depend on a number of different factors:

- The type of product that a business makes
- The needs of different consumer groups
- The level of competition in the market
- The resources available to the business

Quick test

1. Explain why markets change.
2. Explain how technology causes markets to change.
3. Discuss the different ways in which customer behaviour has changed in recent years.
4. Give three ways of segmenting a market.
5. Why do managers segment their target market?

Market-orientated businesses

A business that focuses on making goods and services that **customers want** is considered **market-orientated**. This is the opposite of **product orientation**. Such firms will use market research to find out about the needs of their customers.

Primary research and secondary research

	Benefits	Limitations
Primary research – data gathered by a firm for a specific purpose.	• Data is focused precisely on the issues to be investigated.	• Data can be time-consuming to gather. • Data can be expensive to gather.
Secondary research – data that has already been gathered and published in some form.	• Data can potentially be gathered and analysed quickly.	• Data might be out-of-date. • Data is not specifically tailored for a company's market.

Methods of primary research

- Postal questionnaire – a document containing a series of questions is posted to a sample of potential consumers. This method can be relatively cheap but it takes a lot of time to collate the data due to the time it takes questionnaires to be delivered and responses to be sent back.
- Online survey – a number of websites offer firms a service whereby they can design questionnaires and send them to people electronically. These sites often include software that can carry out analysis of the data gathered.
- Interviews – a researcher speaks to people, either face-to-face or on the phone. This can allow for more in-depth investigations than a survey because the interviewer can adapt their questions to probe issues raised by the interviewee. On the other hand, this can be time-consuming because of the time needed to speak to each individual and type up results.
- Focus groups – a sample of people from the target market are gathered for a discussion about a number of topics, such as their perceptions of different brands. Their responses are noted. This is a faster process than phone interviews but it can produce distorted results if someone in the focus group has strong opinions on a topic.

Revision tip

Can you think of any online tools that can be used by business owners? How would they help speed up the process of gathering primary data?

Revision tip

How do you think the research carried out by the owner of a small business would be different to that carried out by the owner of a micro business? Why do you think that is?

The need for sampling

Interviewing or surveying everyone in your target market would be very expensive and would take a long time. This is why market researchers tend to examine a sample of people from the market. By looking at the views and opinions of people who are **representative** of the wider market, it is possible to get an accurate picture of the needs of most customers in the market at a lower cost and in less time.

Methods of secondary research

- Online – there are a number of different sources of data online that can be useful to firms. Trade associations publish reports about the market for their products. Local and national governments publish economic and demographic data. Companies publish their annual reports online. This can allow researchers to collect large amounts of data quickly, but they have to be careful that the source of the data is valid and reliable. Some people publish information that is highly biased or entirely fake and, to an untrained eye, this can look very much like the real thing.
- Accessing government sources – government departments publish data on a range of different topics. Many governments publish data on the economy, such as predictions for interest rates and **exchange rates**. This data can be downloaded and analysed by market researchers, often at no cost.
- Paying for commercial market research reports – large organisations such as Mintel and Key Note produce market research reports on a range of topics. These reports can be bought by anyone, but can cost thousands of dollars.

Factors influencing the accuracy of market research data

The accuracy of market research can be affected by a number of different factors:

- How it was collected; for example, the method of research and the **sampling** strategy used.
- How recently it was collected; for example, in the market for fashion, which changes frequently, data might become invalid in a matter of weeks.
- Who collected it; for example, organisations that promote the rights of smokers publish data that minimises the health risks of smoking and emphasises the rights of smokers to be able to pursue their habit.

Quick test

1. Name two different types of market research.
2. Describe two different methods of carrying out market research.
3. Explain why it is important to plan sampling carefully when you carry out market research.
4. Discuss the factors that influence the accuracy of the market research carried out by a firm.

Analyse market research data

Graphs

A bar graph can be used to show the number of people that fall into certain categories, for example, the different number of **customers** in each age group. This can help make judgements about the relative size of different groups.

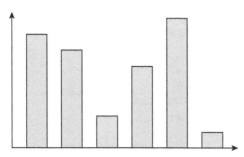

Line graphs can show changes in data from one point in time to another. This can help marketers spot trends, such as increases or decreases in the number of customers who buy certain products.

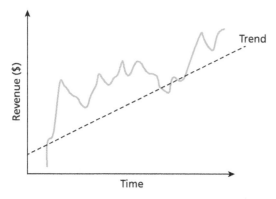

Charts

Pie charts can be used to show the proportion of different groups that are interested in something. They are commonly used by marketers to show the relative size of market segments.

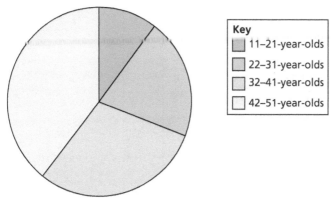

Key
- 11–21-year-olds
- 22–31-year-olds
- 32–41-year-olds
- 42–51-year-olds

You must be able to:
- outline a range of methods of analysing market data
- consider marketing research in order to come to conclusions about marketing activity.

> **Revision tip**
>
> Line graphs are often used to display time series data – data that shows how something has changed over a period of months or even years.

A scattergraph shows the relationship between two variables, for example, if there is a **correlation** between the price of a product and the number of people who want to buy it.

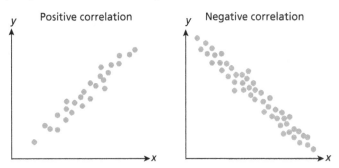

Draw simple conclusions from such data

By visualising data in the form of graphs and charts, it becomes easier for marketers to identify patterns and to spot relationships between different points.

Quick test

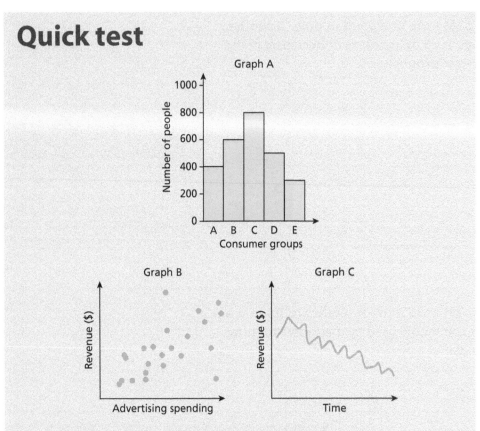

1. In graph A, which consumer group is smallest?
2. What does graph B tell you about the relationship between revenue and advertising spending?
3. How would you describe the trend in sales revenue in graph C?

New product development is important for a lot of firms. Many businesses develop a product portfolio that contains a range of goods and services that are at different stages in their **product lifecycle** to ensure that the business has a chance to be **competitive** in the current market environment and in the future.

The costs and benefits of developing new products

Costs of new product development	Benefits of developing new products
• Research and development is expensive. • This process can be time-consuming. • There is no guarantee of success. • Firms that are first to launch an innovative product might find that other firms copy their ideas after their product is launched.	• New products might allow the firm to meet the needs of existing customers or attract new groups of customers. • New products allow firms to reduce the risks of existing products failing.

Brand image

When a company creates a brand for their business this is often associated with a particular image. A successful brand can be placed on a range of different products and any positive views that people hold about one product will be transferred onto other goods in their portfolio.

The impact of brand image on sales and customer loyalty

A product with a successful brand can often be sold for a higher price because customers are willing to pay more for what they see as higher quality goods. This can lead to higher sales revenue.

A brand also helps to **differentiate** one product from others on the market and could therefore increase sales because customers will be more likely to recognise and want the branded product.

The role of packaging

Packaging can give messages to customers about the product. For example, if packaging is elaborate or made of certain materials, customers are more likely to perceive a product as being of better quality. For example, drinks in glass bottles tend to be seen as of a higher quality than drinks in plastic bottles.

The product lifecycle

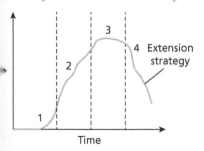

	Main stages and extension strategies	How stages of the product lifecycle can influence marketing decisions
1	Introduction – when new products are launched. There are unlikely to be many competitors at this stage, but the firm will most likely have low revenues from only selling a few items. Firms are likely to have a **negative cashflow** at this stage.	Large amounts of **promotion** are needed as the target market is unlikely to be aware of the product. In some cases, the price will be lower than usual to encourage a product trial by customers.
2	Growth – the number of items sold and the revenue earned is increasing. More competitors are likely to be entering the market. Firms may begin to achieve a **positive cashflow** during this stage.	The number of competitors increases as the number of potential customers rises. Firms may have to increase their spending on promotion during this stage. Many firms will choose a **competitive pricing** strategy at this stage. Decisions relating to place will be important, with the most successful products fighting for the best distribution channels.
3	Maturity – revenue, and the number of items sold are likely to have peaked. Most potential customers have already bought the product and very few (if any) new customers will be entering the market. The number of competitors in the market is also likely to have peaked. Firms are likely to have a positive cashflow at this stage.	At this stage the product will be well established in the market and less **advertising** is likely to be needed. Promotional activity will be focused on retaining existing customers. This might mean promotional methods such as direct marketing.
4	Decline – revenue, and the number of sales, begin to decline. Competitors start to exit the market. The firm needs to focus on cutting costs to continue making a profit.	At this stage, the focus is on keeping costs to a minimum, and so the firm will focus on spending the lowest possible amount on promotion, unless it wants to implement an extension strategy.

Extension strategies

Sometimes, a product has reached the decline stage and sales have started to fall. In some cases, it is possible to reverse this decline in sales through the use of an **extension strategy** that will create growth in sales. This often involves a promotional campaign to encourage customers to buy the product again, or a decision to target the product at a different market segment.

Quick test

1. What is the product lifecycle?
2. Name the stages in the product lifecycle.
3. At which stage in the product lifecycle is a business likely to spend less money on promotion?
4. At which stage in the product lifecycle are competitors likely to leave the market?

Marketing mix: price

Pricing methods

Pricing method	Benefits	Limitations
Cost-plus – when a desired profit margin is added to the cost of producing a good or service	- Simple because it requires no specialist knowledge to apply	- Does not take into account the needs of consumers or market conditions
Competitive – when goods are sold at or about the same price as those of a firm's competitors	- Reduces the chances of a competitor's products being chosen instead	- A firm may have to lower its prices if its competitors lower their prices, which could reduce revenues from sales
Penetration – when a low price is charged when a product is first launched; the price is then raised to its intended level once it is established in the market	- Can stimulate a product trial by consumers	- Could lower the perceived value of a product if the price is left too low for too long
Price skimming – when a high price is charged when a product is first launched and then reduced once **early adopters** have all bought the product	- Allows a higher profit margin on sales to customers willing to pay more as the first to buy it	- Could damage the value of a brand if customers feel the business is being greedy - Competitors might launch their products at a lower price
Promotional – when prices are reduced as a special offer; common forms are "Buy one, get one free" or 50 per cent off	- Can lead to short-term increases in revenue - Can encourage people to try a product	- Does not create customer loyalty – once the offer ends, customers will buy whatever is cheapest

Recommend and justify an appropriate pricing method in given circumstances

The type of pricing that a business uses will depend on a number of factors:

- The intended positioning of the product in the market – for example, whether it is meant to be seen as high or low quality
- The level of competition in the market
- The level of demand in the market

Understand the significance of price elasticity

When the demand for a product is **price elastic** this means that customers are very sensitive to changes in the price of that product. If the price goes up then the demand for the product will go down by a proportionally larger amount.

If a product has **inelastic demand**, the opposite is true: when the price of a product goes up, demand will fall by a proportionately smaller amount.

Companies wanting to make more revenue should bear in mind that a lower price will lead to:

- lower revenue if the product has **inelastic demand**
- higher revenue if the product has **elastic demand**.

Quick test

1. List three pricing strategies that a business could use.
2. List three things that a business should take into account when setting its prices.
3. Why is it important to consider price elasticity when setting prices?

Marketing mix: place

Distribution channels

A **distribution channel** is how a business gets its products to market. It can involve a number of different stages. The fewer stages that a business includes in its distribution channel, the more potential profit will be available to the business.

Advantages and disadvantages of different channels

You must be able to:
• outline a range of different distribution channels
• explain the advantages and disadvantages of different distribution channels
• justify recommendations for appropriate distribution channels in different circumstances.

Distribution channel	Advantages	Disadvantages
Wholesalers – large firms that sell to smaller businesses such as retailers or cafés; they buy goods in bulk and break them down into smaller quantities to be sold.	• Wholesalers deal with many small retailers, whose products benefit from a wider distribution with less work.	• Wholesalers want to make a profit when they sell goods on, as do the retailers they sell to, meaning a lower price can be charged.
Retailers – businesses that sell goods directly to customers; the largest chains such as Carrefour in Europe and Walmart in the USA tend to buy directly from manufacturers.	• Large retail chains are likely to buy and sell large quantities of goods, leading to higher revenues.	• Large chains might demand discounts for purchasing in large quantities.
Direct to customers – some businesses sell their goods directly to customers; sometimes this is small firms using online platforms such as Etsy; sometimes this is larger firms such as Apple, which sells its phones directly to consumers.	• Complete control over how products are sold, for example, standards of **customer service**. • A larger profit margin as there are no **intermediaries** in the distribution channel.	• Requires the business to set up facilities to deal with customer orders, returns and ongoing service. • Can be a distraction for managers from core activities such as designing and making products.

> **Revision tip**
>
> If you were the owner of a manufacturing business, would you rather sell goods directly to customers or through an intermediary? Why?

Recommend and justify an appropriate distribution channel in given circumstances

The most appropriate **distribution channel** for your business will depend on a number of different factors, including:

- what kind of image you want to create for your product, for example, the image of luxury goods would be spoiled if they were sold by discount retailers
- how much control you want over the sale of your product
- how much profit you are aiming to make – the more intermediaries there are in the supply chain, the less profit you will make.

Quick test

1. What is a distribution channel?
2. Why do some businesses try to remove intermediaries from their distribution channels?
3. What should a manufacturer take into account when a choosing a new distribution channel?

The aims of promotion

When businesses promote their goods and services, they might aim to achieve a number of different goals.

- Raising awareness – they might want to increase the number of people who know about their product or who can recognise their brand.
- To increase sales – the business might use promotional techniques to sell a greater number of goods and services.
- To reinforce purchase decisions – some industries, such as car manufacturers, aim to reassure customers that they made the right decision by purchasing their brand.
- To inform and educate – charities and public sector firms might want people to learn about a specific issue, such as a way of preventing a health problem, or to let them know about a crisis in a foreign country.

Different forms of promotion and how they influence sales

- **Advertising** – this involves paying for space in a media channel to share a message with **consumers**. The more people the advert is likely to reach, the higher the cost of the advert. For example, adverts during the Super Bowl in the USA cost hundreds of millions of dollars but they also reach an audience of hundreds of millions of people.
  Other, cheaper forms of advertising can be useful because, while they might reach a smaller number of customers, they are more likely to be read by specific market segments, for example, advertising in certain newspapers or magazines, or before a film starts in a cinema. These forms of advertising benefit from lower **production** costs.
- **Sales promotion** – This is when a business uses discounts and special offers to encourage customers to make a purchase. This can be a useful method of increasing revenue in the short term if a product has price **inelastic demand**, but is unlikely to gain your business customers in the long term.

The need for cost effectiveness in spending the marketing budget on promotion

It is important to get good value for money when paying for promotional activity. It might be an attractive idea to have an advert reach a million people, but if only one of those people is ever likely to buy your product, you are getting very poor value for money. In such circumstances, other methods such as personal selling might be more appropriate.

Quick test

1. What does the term 'promotion' mean?
2. What is the difference between advertising and sales promotion?
3. Why is it important to consider cost effectiveness when choosing promotional activities?

Technology and the marketing mix

Define and explain the concept of e-commerce

E-commerce is when some or all of the activities of a business are conducted using the internet. This might mean **online advertising** using social networks like Facebook; it could also mean selling goods directly to customers, either through your own **transactional website** or using a platform such as Amazon or eBay.

The opportunities and threats of e-commerce to businesses and consumers

Online businesses have lower costs than traditional **bricks and mortar** companies. This is because they have more flexibility to locate their premises in areas where land and rent are cheaper. Also, because a large company like Amazon buys huge quantities of goods from **suppliers**, they might be able to secure lower costs when purchasing stock. This could mean that they can charge customers lower prices, outcompeting traditional firms.

On the other hand, online firms depend on delivery companies. If an online business is not able to get goods to customers in a reasonable amount of time, this might lead **consumers** to believe that it makes more sense to go to a bricks and mortar shop and pay a higher price and receive their purchases straight away.

Use of the internet and social media networks for promotion

A famous advertiser once said: "Half of my advertising **budget** is wasted, but I don't know which half!". This was because firms did not know which of their customers had seen traditional adverts and which had not. In the internet age, firms can track how many people have clicked on an online advert and, in some cases, can tell exactly who they are and where they are when they click on the advert. This makes it much easier for companies to measure the effectiveness of their adverts.

Social networks such as Facebook use algorithms to review databases of information to work out which of their members would be most interested in specific adverts. This makes advertising on these platforms good value for money for a range of firms.

You must be able to:

- outline the concept of e-commerce
- explain the importance of e-commerce to businesses and consumers
- consider the role of e-commerce within the marketing mix.

Revision tip

Which products do you buy online? Which ones do you buy from traditional retail businesses? Are you buying more or less products from E-commerce companies that you were five years ago?

Quick test

1. Name the elements of the marketing mix.
2. Outline three methods of promotion.
3. Explain how technology impacts upon the design of the marketing mix.

Recommend and justify marketing strategies appropriate to a given situation

The marketing strategies that a business uses will depend on a range of issues, including:

- the marketing strategies used by competing firms
- the tastes and preferences of customers
- the economic environment in which the firm operates.

The importance of different elements of the marketing mix in influencing consumer decisions in given circumstances

Each element of the **marketing mix** has the potential to influence **consumers** in different ways:

- The promotional methods used can inform customers about the uses of a product and the features it contains. This might encourage them to buy goods or purchase them in larger quantities.
- Pricing can influence the perceptions of customers. Goods that are sold at a premium price might be seen as higher **quality** than other products.
- Product is important because if firms do not develop new versions of their products then they might be seen as out of date.
- Place is important because if products are sold through certain **distribution channels** such as discount stores, it could damage an upmarket image.

The nature and impact of legal controls related to marketing

The marketing activities of firms are subject to a number of **laws** and **regulations**.

The impact of legal controls on marketing strategy

Misleading promotion – firms are not allowed to make statements in their adverts that are untrue. For example, they cannot claim that products work faster or last longer than they actually do.

Faulty and dangerous goods – consumer protection laws make it illegal for firms to sell products that are not fit for their intended purpose. Customers are entitled to remedies such as a refund or a replacement.

> **Revision tip**
>
> Look for examples in newspapers of stories about consumers enforcing their rights. This should help you to understand the impact of legal controls more clearly and give you some examples that you can use in exam answers.

Quick test

1. Name one factor that will influence the type of marketing strategy chosen by a firm.
2. Give two ways in which the marketing mix can be used to influence the opinions of customers.
3. Give one legal control on marketing activity.

The opportunities and problems of entering new foreign markets

Growth potential of new markets in other countries

International expansion is attractive to many firms because it offers the chance to sell goods to large numbers of people that may never have bought their product before. This can offer an opportunity to increase the size of a business and therefore increase the profits that the business makes.

Problems of entering foreign markets

- **Cultural differences** – **culture** is the shared norms and values that people hold in a particular place. It is about the way the people believe they should behave. This has led many companies to adapt their products for local markets. For example, to Hindus, the cow is a sacred animal, therefore McDonald's do not sell beef burgers in Indian restaurants.
- **Lack of knowledge** – companies may not understand local cultures, local laws or local business practices. This means that companies will struggle to successfully operate in other countries. In order to get around this problem, many firms hire an agent to support their expansion into these countries.

Benefits and limitations of methods to overcome such problems

- **Joint ventures** – this is when a business enters a foreign market in partnership with another firm, usually one based locally. This means that the risk of international expansion is shared, but the businesses also have to share any profits made. Rules on foreign ownership of companies have meant that a lot of Western firms have set up joint ventures in order to expand into China.
- **Licensing** – this is when a firm is given a licence to produce and distribute products. This is the method that Coca-Cola has used to expand into countries outside the USA. Companies buy a licence to manufacture and distribute Coca-Cola. For example, Coca-Cola is sold in Columbia and India by companies that have bought a licence to bottle and sell the drink.

> **You must be able to:**
> - explain the benefits of entering foreign markets
> - explain the problems involved in entering foreign markets.

Revision tip

The best way to remember culture is to think about it as "The way we do things around here". What are the normal behaviours in your area that might not be observed by someone from abroad? How would this make you feel?

Quick test

1. Why do businesses choose to enter foreign markets?
2. What does the term 'culture' mean?
3. How does a lack of knowledge about local customs impact on a business trying to open a new factory in a foreign country?
4. What is a joint venture?
5. Why might firms choose licensing as a way to enter foreign markets?

Exam-style practice questions

1 Haliva is a train company, operating in the south of country C. The company offers a range of services to meet the needs of its customers. Many passengers on the trains travel for business purposes. Although these travellers consume the service, their employer is the firm's customer, paying for the tickets.

The company operates a specialist service, offering overnight services into neighbouring countries. This service appeals to specific niche markets. As incomes in country C have changed, the market for the rail services has also changed. Passenger numbers have decreased due to increasing car ownership. The company wishes to segment their market more effectively to identify opportunities to maximise revenues. The directors of the company are considering using demographic segmentation.

a) Define the term 'customer needs'. [2]

b) Outline the difference between customers and consumers. [2]

c) Outline the benefits to Haliva of targeting niche markets. [4]

d) Explain two factors that might cause the market for train travel to change. [6]

e) Do you think that demographic segmentation is the most appropriate method of market segmentation for Haliva? Justify your answer. [6]

2 Exciting Events is a company which organises concerts by popular bands in country C. The business has become successful in recent years. Primary market research conducted by the company has indicated that many of their customers now spend less money on recorded music because of online streaming. They spend the money that they save on concert tickets and merchandise.

The managing director of Exciting Events believes that the research conducted by his staff is accurate because they use a large sample; when carrying out research, they carefully organise people into groups to represent all of the different types of customers; and all research has been carried out recently.

The Exciting Events business is focusing on developing its merchandising operations. Years ago, music fans simply bought T-shirts and programmes to commemorate concerts. Now they spend hundreds of dollars on a range of merchandise. The managing director believes that this business is in the growth stage of the product lifecycle. The business currently uses a premium pricing strategy for its merchandise – because customers are often loyal fans of the bands and performers, there is no competition for sales of the merchandise within the concert venues, and because customers who have enjoyed an event are less likely to be price sensitive.

Demand for tickets is inelastic with many customers paying large sums of money to see their favourite acts. Some shows do not sell out. The managing director is concerned that this is because the business uses the wrong distribution channels. He is planning to launch a promotional campaign to encourage more customers to use one of the two existing distribution channels – face-to-face sales via a box office at music venues, or online sales via a specialist ticket-selling business.

a) Explain four methods of carrying out primary research. [8]

b) Explain why the following three factors might contribute to the accuracy of the primary research gathered:

- large samples

- making sure that samples represent the target market

- having research that has been carried out recently.

Which factor is most important? Justify your answer. [12]

c) Explain two implications of having a product in the growth stage of the product lifecycle. [8

d) Explain why the following three factors are important to successfully using a premium pricing strategy:

- customer loyalty

- lack of competition

- price insensitive customers.

Which factor do you think is most important? Justify your answer. [12

e) Explain four factors that might lead to a product having inelastic demand. [8

f) Consider the two options that the managing director has proposed:

- selling more tickets direct to customers via box offices

- selling more tickets to customers through third-party ticket agencies.

Which option should the managing director focus on? Justify your answer. [12

Managing resources effectively to produce goods and services

An operations manager is responsible for organising staff and machinery to ensure that **raw materials** are transformed into goods and services in the most efficient way possible. Operations managers are responsible for ensuring the highest possible rate of **productivity** for a business.

Difference between production and productivity

Production is the goods a business makes or the services it provides. Productivity is the rate at which machines and employees are able to produce goods and services. The higher the rate of productivity, the more production will be completed each day.

Benefits of increasing efficiency and how to increase it

- Increasing productivity by **automation** and technology – in modern factories, machines can do larger quantities of work more accurately than humans ever could. For example, robotic arms can pack goods on production lines into boxes with speed and accuracy. This type of technology has spread to other sectors. For example, in the retail sector self-service tills allow more transactions to be processed with far fewer staff.
- Improved labour skills – by training workers, it is possible to make them more productive. This is because people who have more skills are able to complete more tasks and more sophisticated tasks than employees who are not as well trained.

Why businesses hold inventories

Businesses hold stock, or inventory, so that they can satisfy the needs of customers and cope with unexpected changes in the level of demand. This is because there is a **lead time** on deliveries from **suppliers**. The lead time might be a number of days or weeks. Firms tend to hold **inventories** that will last at least long enough to order more stock from their suppliers.

The concept of lean production

Lean production is a **quality** management philosophy focused on eliminating waste from the workplace, producing the largest possible quantity of goods or services with the smallest quantity of waste. This could be any kind of waste:

- Wasted motion by workers is eliminated by reorganising workplaces to minimise the amount of movement necessary.
- Wasted working hours are eliminated by redesigning jobs.
- Wasted **raw materials** are eliminated by controlling quality standards in the workplace carefully.

You must be able to:
- outline the issues involved in producing goods and services
- explain the benefits of increasing efficiency in the production process
- explain the benefits of lean production to a range of firms.

 Revision tip

How would learning better skills make you better at your work as a student? If you learned to make notes more quickly, how much more efficiently would you use your time?

 Revision tip

Observe your fellow students in your study areas or classrooms. Can you see any examples of wasted time or motion? Try to think about how lean production could make you a more efficient learner.

How to achieve lean production

The following are two examples:

- **Just in time (JIT) inventory control** is a system whereby a business holds just enough stock to last until the next delivery arrives. This means that more space can be used for production, and less space and resources are needed for storage. This improves the overall **productivity** of a business although it does rely on having reliable **suppliers**. Unlike traditional stock control systems, a JIT inventory control system will not require any buffer stocks.

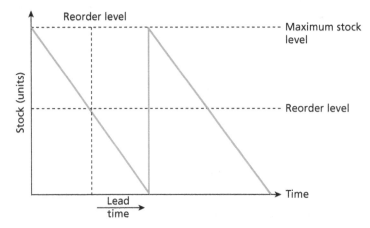

- **Kaizen** is the Japanese phrase for 'change for better'. It is a management philosophy of continually improving the processes and procedures used in a business. This means that small improvements are constantly made to work practices, and the views of all members of staff on possible improvements are considered to be important.

Benefits of lean production

- Costs are reduced as a result of reducing waste, potentially allowing businesses to make greater profits.
- Resources are used more efficiently, increasing levels of **productivity** and leading to higher levels of output.
- Workers are involved in the **quality** improvements, leading to greater levels of empowerment and **motivation** amongst workers.

Quick test

1. Explain the difference between production and productivity.
2. Explain the meaning of the term 'efficiency'.
3. Name two lean production techniques.
4. Discuss the benefits of lean production to firms producing goods and services.

The main methods of production

Features, benefits and limitations of job, batch and flow production

Features	Benefits	Limitations
Job production – products are made as a one-off, according to the needs of customers.	<ul><li>Products can be tailored to the needs of customers.</li><li>Only the products that are needed are made.</li><li>Production relies on the skill of workers, which can be motivational.</li></ul>	<ul><li>Goods are not produced in sufficient quantities to gain economies of scale.</li><li>It might be hard to find enough workers with the necessary skills.</li></ul>
Batch production – relatively small numbers of similar goods are produced in batches.	<ul><li>The production process can be partially automated, reducing labour costs.</li><li>It is flexible and can be adapted to the needs of different groups of customers.</li></ul>	<ul><li>Set-up costs can be high because machinery is expensive.</li></ul>
Flow production – identical products are produced continuously, often using a production line.	<ul><li>Firms can achieve economies of scale by purchasing large quantities of raw materials.</li><li>Production is highly mechanised and therefore requires lower labour costs.</li></ul>	<ul><li>There is no scope to tailor products to individual requirements.</li><li>If a production line breaks, no goods can be made until it is repaired.</li></ul>

> **Revision tip**
>
> Next time you visit your favourite fast-food restaurant, watch the workers making the food. Which method of production are they using to make the food? What method is used when customers have a special requirement?

How technology has changed production methods

Changes in technology have led to vast improvements in the **productivity** of production processes. Many modern firms use **CADCAM** systems, which can allow highly cost-effective production of small quantities of goods. Methods such as additive manufacturing (also known as 3D printing) allow firms to produce prototypes and even finished goods in small quantities.

Quick test

1. List three methods of production.
2. Give two advantages of batch production.
3. Give two drawbacks of flow production.
4. Explain how technology has changed the production methods used by firms.

As companies grow, they produce larger quantities of goods and services. As more goods and services are produced, production costs can be spread over a larger number of units of output. The result of this is that production costs per unit are lower. This is known as **economies of scale**.

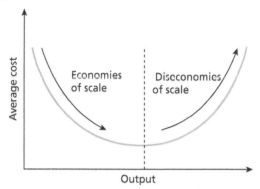

Types of economy of scale

- Purchasing – buying larger quantities of **raw materials** means that firms can obtain discounts for purchasing in larger quantities. This in turn makes the cost of producing goods lower.
- Marketing – as a larger firm promotes its brand in addition to its products, more people are able to recognise that brand. When the brand is applied to new products, this leads to lower costs of **promotion** for the new products; customers may not be familiar with the new products, but they will know the brand, which reduces the amount of money the firm needs to spend on promotion.
- Financial – a larger firm is able to get a better deal on credit from banks. As a firm gets bigger, it is able to borrow money at lower interest rates. Therefore, the ongoing costs of repaying loans is reduced.
- Managerial – as a firm gets bigger, it is able to hire specialist workers who can focus on tasks such as marketing, finance and human resources management. These specialist managers and staff are able to work more efficiently than entrepreneurs who try to do all of these jobs themselves. This added **efficiency** increases **productivity** and therefore reduces costs.
- Technical – as a business grows, it is able to purchase machinery that allows it to partially or fully automate production processes. This allows larger quantities of goods to be made with less waste and less labour. This decreases the cost of production and increases **productivity** as fewer workers are needed to produce each unit of finished goods, and machines can often produce goods at a faster pace without taking any breaks.

Scale of production

The concept of diseconomies of scale

While businesses gain economies of scale as they grow, it is possible for a business to grow too large. Past a certain level of growth, the unit cost of producing goods and services will begin to increase as problems begin to emerge.

Types of diseconomy of scale

- **Poor communication** – in a larger firm it can get harder to communicate between different branches that are dispersed over different geographical areas, possibly in different countries. Firms in overseas locations might find that their staff speak a different language to staff in the head office. Workers in different time zones might struggle to co-ordinate suitable times for meetings.
- **Lack of commitment from employees** – in a smaller firm where staff know one another and are likely to know the owners of the business as well, they are likely to be more motivated and therefore more productive. As a business grows, workers are increasingly less likely to feel like they are a part of the organisation and are more likely to feel anonymous. This may produce demotivation, which will lead to lower **productivity** and therefore higher costs.
- **Weak co-ordination** – in a larger firm, when managers have a larger **span of control** or there are many layers of management, it can take a long time for messages to be passed on. This might mean that it takes longer for activities to start. Workers in different areas might be working to different standards and in different ways. This will lead to inconsistencies in the standards of different parts of the business, creating waste and thereby increasing costs.

Quick test

1. Define mass production.
2. Give two benefits of batch production.
3. Explain the meaning of the term 'economies of scale'.
4. Describe two different ways of achieving economies of scale.
5. Discuss the impact of diseconomies of scale on a range of businesses.

Classifying costs

- **Fixed** – these costs do not change as the number of customers served increases. An example of a fixed cost might be the repayments on a mortgage for a factory or the cost of repayments of a loan used to buy machinery.
- **Variable** – these costs are linked to the level of production in a business. They rise as more goods are produced or more customers are served. Examples of **variable costs** might include the cost of raw materials or the cost of packaging each item. The variable costs of a business can be calculated using the following formula:
Variable costs per unit × number of units produced = variable costs
- **Average** – this is when the costs of producing goods or services are divided by the number of items produced. As a firm produces more units, these costs decrease. This is known as economies of scale.
(fixed costs + variable costs) ÷ output = average cost per unit.
- **Total** – total costs are the sum of fixed costs and variable costs. Total costs can be subtracted from total revenue to calculate profit or divided by output to calculate the average cost per unit.

Use cost data to help make simple cost-based decisions

Cost data can help business owners decide when to stop or continue production. If variable costs are higher than the selling price of a product, this means that there will be a loss made when the product is sold. At this point owners should consider either taking steps to reduce costs, for example, finding a cheaper supplier, or stopping production of that product so that resources can be focused on goods that will make profits.

Quick test

Answer questions 1–3 based on this data:

Variable cost per unit:	$5
Fixed costs:	$800
Units sold:	200

1. What are the total variable costs for this product?
2. What are the total costs for this product?
3. What are the average costs per unit for this product?

Break-even analysis

The concept of break-even

Break-even output is the number of products that a firm has to sell in order to cover its costs. Every item that it sells after reaching the break-even point contributes to its profits. The break-even point is reached when total costs are equal to total revenue. At this point, the firm is making neither a profit nor a loss.

Break-even output is always stated as the number of goods or services sold. This is why it is also known as the break-even level of output.

Interpret a break-even chart

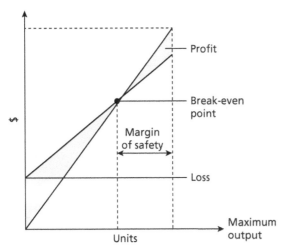

Revision tip

Make sure that you can remember the formulae and how to label the different areas on the break-even graph. Try to practise as many calculations as possible for this topic.

Calculate break-even output

The break-even level of output can be calculated using the following formulae:

selling price – variable costs = contribution

fixed costs ÷ contribution = break-even output

Define, calculate and interpret the margin of safety

The **margin of safety** is the difference between the break-even level of output and the actual output at a firm. This is the number of sales that a business can lose without making a loss.

The margin of safety can be calculated using the formula:

actual output – break-even output = margin of safety

Use break-even analysis to help make simple decisions

Break-even analysis can be used to examine the impact of changes to costs, and the impact of a higher price. By calculating the new break-even level of output when costs or prices change, it is possible for managers to see the impact of a change and make a decision about new sales targets in light of these changes.

Break-even analysis:

- only applies to one product at a time
- does not take into account changes in the external environment, such as increases in the cost of **raw materials**
- is useful as a tool for planning and setting targets, but it does not guarantee that the break-even level of output will be achieved.

Quick test

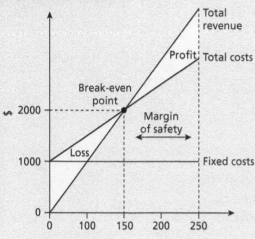

1. Explain the term 'margin of safety'.
2. How many items must be sold for this firm to break even?
3. What is the maximum output for this firm?
4. Assuming the firm is operating at its maximum capacity, what is its margin of safety?
5. How much are the fixed costs for this firm?
6. What is the selling price per unit for this firm?
7. Using the following data, construct a break-even chart:

Fixed costs	$600
Variable cost per unit	$2
Selling price	$5
Maximum output	350 units

Label the following points on the graph:
- Margin of safety
- Break-even point
- Area of profit
- Area of loss
- Maximum output

8. Explain two factors that limit the usefulness of break-even analysis.

Why quality is important and how quality production might be achieved

What quality means and why it is important for all businesses

Quality refers to the standards that a business achieves in its goods and in the service that it provides to customers. The higher these standards are, the better the quality of the products or services that it provides.

Quality is important because it can provide a source of differentiation for businesses, with companies that offer higher quality standing out from their competitors. Quality is also important because if a firm achieves higher standards, it is able to charge higher, premium prices.

There are two main ways that businesses manage the quality of their goods and services: through **quality control** and **quality assurance**.

The concept of quality control and how businesses implement quality control

Quality control is when goods and services are inspected at the end of the production process. A sample of the goods produced will be checked by an inspector and if any errors are found, they are corrected; if no errors are found, the goods are sent out to customers.

The concept of quality assurance and how this can be implemented

Quality assurance is when goods are continually checked throughout the production process. In a business with a quality assurance culture, the responsibility for quality belongs to every employee in the firm. Any worker can stop production if they see a problem with the standard of the goods being produced.

You must be able to:
- outline the importance of managing quality
- explain the difference between quality assurance and quality control.

> **Revision tip**

When was the last time that you bought goods or services which were not of good quality? How did you react? Have you been back to that business since? Why?

Quick test

1. Explain two benefits of managing the quality of goods and services produced by a firm.
2. Explain the difference between quality control and quality assurance.

The main factors influencing the location and relocation decisions of a business

Factors relevant to the location decision of manufacturing businesses and service businesses

When the owners of a business are considering the best possible location for their premises, they should examine a number of factors:

- Proximity to **suppliers** – if a business is close to its suppliers, it is able to receive deliveries faster. This can reduce the **lead times** associated with ordering stock, which is useful for firms operating a just in time stock control system.
- Proximity to customers – this is important because a business that is close to customers' homes or workplaces is more convenient for them to visit, and could lead to an increase in footfall – more people will visit the business.
- Proximity to labour – if a business requires a large number of staff, it might want to locate near an area with high unemployment. If a business requires a large number of workers with specific skills, it might locate in an area where a large number of people have experience in their industry. For example, many electronics firms locate in the USA's Silicon Valley because many suitably skilled workers live there.
- Cost of land – businesses that require a large amount of land, such as car factories or hypermarkets, might prefer to locate in areas where land is cheaper to buy. This allows them to create not only shop-floor areas within their premises, but also complementary services, such as car parks for staff and customers.
- Transport links – factories might want to locate near major road networks so that they can easily receive deliveries and transport finished goods to customers quickly. Service businesses might want to locate near roads or railway stations so that it is convenient for customers to visit them.

Factors that a business could consider when deciding in which country to locate operations

Language – the language spoken in the country is an important consideration. Does the business have staff that can communicate with local customers, suppliers and potential employees, or will it need to hire new staff with those language skills?

Culture – What are the accepted patterns of behaviour in the countries under consideration? How do people normally use particular goods and services? For example, in some countries lilies are associated with funerals, so businesses should not decorate their premises with them – unless they are in the funeral business!

> **You must be able to:**
> - outline a range of factors influencing the location of a business
> - explain the importance of different location factors to businesses producing both goods and services.

> **Revision tip**
>
> Use a search engine to find a map of your local area. Pinpoint different types of business on the map and use sticky notes to summarise why those firms might have chosen those locations.

- Demand – Will the population of the target country be willing to buy the goods and services being offered?
- Competition – Does a local firm already offer the same type of goods and services? Is something better or different being offered compared with what established firms are offering?

The role of legal controls on location decisions

When choosing a location, businesses must consider the impact of local laws. In some cases, there might be rules controlling the hours that businesses can open, how long staff can work, the minimum wages that can be paid to staff, or governing the safety of production processes.

The cost of compliance with legal requirements must be considered. For example, an area with low labour costs might still be an expensive place to locate a firm because of rules that state, for example, that a company building a new factory must fund the building of other local facilities such as schools or affordable houses.

Quick test

1. List three factors that should be considered when locating a manufacturing business.

2. Recommend one factor that you believe is most important to the location of a service business.

3. Discuss the factors that you consider most important when choosing an international location for a manufacturing business.

1 Mollie's Cupcakes is a small business, based in country D, which produces freshly baked cakes. The company is highly productive and keeps costs as low as possible using lean management techniques.

Cupcakes are ordered by a range of customers such as small cafés and large department stores. The business makes cakes according to the exact needs of its customers using job production methods.

The company produces thousands of cakes each week, allowing it to gain purchasing economies of scale. This lowers the variable costs of the business, but the company has high fixed costs because of the high rent that it has to pay for its bakery. The company uses break-even analysis to plan production, making sure that the company remains profitable.

a) Define 'productivity'. [2]

b) Define 'lean management'. [2]

c) Outline the benefits of job production to Mollie's cupcakes. [4]

d) Explain two economies of scale that Mollie's cupcakes might be able to achieve. [6]

e) Do you think that break-even analysis is an effective method to ensure that the business remains profitable? Justify your answer. [6]

2 Jimmy's Cricket is a sporting goods supplier which specialises in supplying professional cricket teams in the UK. The business manufactures a range of products in the UK and sells them through a website. In order to minimise costs, it has no physical premises. The business has a large margin of safety as a result of these low costs. The owners believe that this helps them respond more effectively to competitive pressure in the market.

The business prides itself on providing the best products in the world and the owners believe that this is because of their rigorous quality assurance system which means that standards for products are the responsibility of every worker, that products are constantly checked for defects, and that all staff know the standards of quality expected.

Quality has been the unique selling point of the business for over 100 years and the current owners believe that this gives them a significant advantage over their competitors. Another reason that the owners believe that the business is thriving is their central location. The business is near transport links and is close to an area where a lot of skilled craftspeople live.

a) Explain four benefits of a large margin of safety. [8]

b) Explain why the following three factors make quality assurance at Jimmy's Cricket effective:

  – quality being the responsibility of every worker

  – constant checks on products

  – all staff knowing quality standards

  Which factor is most important? Justify your answer. [12]

c) Explain four reasons why a high standard of quality makes a business like Jimmy's Cricket more competitive. [8]

d) Consider the location of the business. It is:

   – near transport links

   – close to a large pool of skilled labour

   Which factor is more important to making the business competitive? Justify your answer. [12

Business finance: needs and sources

The main reasons why businesses need finance

- Start-up capital – cash is needed to open a new business. Premises need to be rented and equipment needs to be bought, employees need to be recruited and trained, and enough stock is required to get up and running.
- Capital for expansion – when a business grows, it needs cash to finance the purchasing of additional equipment, the extension of premises, and the recruitment and training of additional staff.
- Additional working capital – working capital is the money that a business uses from day to day to pay its bills. Sometimes a business needs additional working capital to fund an especially busy time. For example, a restaurant might need extra working capital to buy ingredients if it expects an unusually large number of customers.

> You must be able to:
> - outline different reasons why firms need finance
> - explain the difference between short-term and long-term finance
> - explain the different sources of finance that a firm can choose.

Understand the difference between short-term and long-term finance needs

Short-term finance needs are to provide enough **working capital** to keep a business running from day to day. This could be paying wages to staff or buying stock and raw materials. Short-term finance is usually used to fund **revenue expenditure** – the day-to-day costs of operations.

Long-term finance needs are associated with **capital expenditure** – making long-term investments, such as the purchasing of new machinery or a new building.

The main sources of finance

Internal sources and external sources

Internal sources of finance are those generated from within the business. External finance comes from sources outside the business, such as banks or investors.

Short-term and long-term sources

An **overdraft** is suitable for short-term finance. This is a facility that enables a business to borrow money flexibly on its bank account. There is no fixed amount that is borrowed each month, but there is an overall limit on how much money can be borrowed. This type of finance is usually paid back within a few days or weeks, and a relatively high interest rate is charged.

Debt or **equity** are suitable sources for long-term finance. Debt is when a business borrows money, normally from a bank, in the form of either a loan or a mortgage. Equity is when a business sells shares to investors. The investors then own a portion of the business and are entitled to an annual dividend – a share of any profits made.

Revision tip

Try visiting your local bank to find out the costs and benefits of using different types of loans and overdrafts as a business owner.

Importance of alternative sources of capital

- **Microfinance** – this is when small loans are offered to people who are unemployed or on low incomes and lack the collateral needed to borrow money. Microfinance is available all over the world, but it is most common in developing countries.
- **Crowdfunding** – this is when a business offers their product for sale through a website such as Kickstarter before it has actually been produced. Customers are able to make a commitment to buy the product when it is eventually made. This allows firms to raise money for new and untested ideas that otherwise might not be an attractive investment for traditional investors.

The main factors considered in making the financial choice

- Size and legal form of business – smaller businesses might be less creditworthy because they have fewer assets that could be taken by the bank if the business fails.
- Amount required – the more money you need, the more important it is to use a source of finance with low interest rates. For example, if a firm needs millions of dollars for a large asset such as a factory, a long-term source of finance such as a mortgage is the most appropriate choice.
- Length of time – different sources of finance each have a different repayment term – the length of time over which money borrowed is paid back. Loans are typically for 5 to 10 years. Mortgages are often for 25 to 30 years.
- Existing loans – the more money that a business has borrowed, the less likely it will be able to borrow more in the future. A business that already has high debts has less chance of paying back new debts than a business that has borrowed less.

Quick test

1. Explain why start-up capital is important.
2. Give three reasons why a business might need capital for expansion.
3. Explain the meaning of the term 'working capital'.
4. Discuss the difference between short-term and long-term sources of finance.

Working capital

The concept and importance of working capital

Working capital is the money that a business uses to fund day-to-day operations. It is important that a business has sufficient working capital to fund revenue expenditure. If a business does not have working capital, it might not be able to pay its staff, purchase raw materials or pay running costs such as energy bills.

Why cash is important to a business

Cash is the money that is available to a firm to pay its day-to-day expenses. If a business runs out of cash, it is in danger of becoming insolvent, which could lead to a business having to close down. Cash is a combination of money that belongs to the business, such as revenue, and money that the business has borrowed, such as loan capital or overdraft finance.

What a cashflow forecast is

A **cashflow** forecast is a prediction of the money that will flow into a business, such as revenue and loan capital, and money that flows out of a business, such as wages and loan repayments.

How a cashflow forecast is constructed

	January	February
Inflows	$900	$800
Outflows	$1200	$400
Net cashflow	– $300	$400
Opening balance	$200	–$100
Closing balance	– $100	$300

net cashflow = inflows – outflows

opening balance = previous closing balance

You must be able to:
- outline the importance of working capital
- explain the reasons why firms need to produce a cashflow forecast.

The importance of cashflow

Cashflow forecasting is important to the managers of a business. By predicting when a business might run out of cash, it is possible to arrange appropriate short-term sources of finance so that the business can continue trading.

Quick test

1. Why do managers need to forecast cashflow?
2. How do you calculate net cashflow?
3. If the closing balance on your cashflow forecast for February is $900, what will the opening balance be in March?

Cashflow forecasting

How to amend a simple cashflow forecast

Worked example: before

	January	February
Inflows ($)	25 000	25 000
Outflows ($)	20 000	20 000
Net cashflow ($)	5000	5000
Opening balance ($)	0	5000
Closing balance ($)	5000	10 000

In this example, the business has to change its forecast because it has to buy machinery costing $5000 in February.

This leads to the following changes:

1. Outflows in February increase to $25 000 ($20 000 + $5000)

2. Net cashflow in February falls to $0 ($25 000 − $25 000)

3. The closing balance falls to $5000 ($5000 + $0)

Worked example: after

	January	February
Inflows ($)	25 000	25 000
Outflows ($)	20 000	25 000
Net cashflow ($)	5000	0
Opening balance ($)	0	5000
Closing balance ($)	5000	5000

> ### Revision tip
>
> Practice makes perfect – try searching the internet for cashflow activities so that you have plenty of practice performing these calculations.

How to interpret a simple cashflow forecast

	January	February	March	April
Inflows ($)	10 000	12 000	15 000	12 000
Outflows ($)	9000	13 000	18 000	8000
Net cashflow ($)	1000	− 1000	− 3000	4000
Opening balance ($)	2000	3000	2000	− 1000
Closing balance ($)	3000	2000	− 1000	3000

How a short-term cashflow problem might be overcome

- Increasing loans – by borrowing more money from banks or other lenders such as crowdfunding sites, it is possible to inject cash into a business to cover day-to-day running expenses.
- Delaying payments – some suppliers allow a firm to pay their bills at the end of the month rather than straight away. It might be possible for managers to negotiate a longer period of time to pay bills. In some cases, it is possible to agree credit terms of 90 or 120 days. This means that a business has more cash in the short term, but it creates a potential problem in the future: when will it be able to pay its suppliers?
- Asking debtors to pay more quickly – if a business gives its customers credit terms, it might be possible to encourage them to pay their bills sooner than originally planned. This will provide an earlier inflow of cash into the business.

Quick test

Based on the cashflow forecast for January to April on page 74:

1. In which month does the business need to use an overdraft?
2. How could you prevent the business from needing to use an overdraft?
3. When does the business have a negative net cashflow?
4. When does the business have a negative opening balance?

Income statements – what profit is and why it is important

How a profit is made

Profit is made when a business has paid all of its costs and still has money remaining from its revenues:

Profit = revenue – costs

If revenue is greater than total costs, a business has made a profit.

You must be able to:
- explain the purpose of an income statement
- interpret an income statement
- consider an income statement in order to make business decisions.

Importance of profit to private sector businesses

- Reward for risk-taking/enterprise – when an entrepreneur sets up a business, they do so in order to make money. Profits are the money that an entrepreneur is able to take away from their business as a reward for the risks that they take in starting the business.
  In the case of larger firms such as a PLC, profit is the reward that is available to investors. Part of the profits made by a **limited company** are divided up into dividends for each shareholder. This is the reward that they receive for the risk they take in making an investment.
- Source of finance – profit is a source of finance for businesses. At the end of the year, any profits not given to the owners of the firm can be retained by the business for investment in the coming year.

Difference between profit and cash

Profit is the money that belongs to the owners of a business. **Cash** is the money that is available for spending on the running of a business. Cash can include retained profits, revenues, **equity** from shareholders, or money from loans provided by banks or other financiers.

Debt and equity do not belong to the business and so cannot be counted towards the profits made. Only revenues count towards the profits made by a business.

Income statements

An **income statement** is a financial document produced by firms that shows how much money the business has earned, how much it has spent, and how much profit it has made in a year.

Main features of an income statement

- **Revenue** – this is the money that the business earns from selling its goods and services.
- **Cost of sales** – this is the money that has been spent in order to earn revenues. These are costs such as raw materials and the wages of production staff.
- **Gross profit** – this is the money remaining after a business has deducted the cost of sales from its revenues.
- **Profit** – this is the money that remains after a business has deducted its fixed costs from its gross profits.

> **Revision tip**
>
> Try to remember that income statements show the money coming in and out of a business as part of its trading activity.

- **Retained profit** – after a business pays its **taxes** and distributes dividends to its shareholders, the money remaining is retained profit, which can be invested into the running of the business in the future.

Use simple income statements in decision-making based on profit calculations

An **income statement** shows the difference between the total income of a firm and its total costs.

- The income of a firm is its total revenue – all of the money earned from selling goods and services.
- The cost of sales is deducted from total revenue to calculate gross profit. Cost of sales are the costs associated with making a product or service such as raw materials.
- Fixed costs are deducted from gross profits in order to calculate profit. Fixed costs are the overheads incurred in running the business, such as the cost of renting premises.
- When completing an income statement, negative numbers are often illustrated using brackets instead of a minus sign. When a gross profit or profit figure is negative, this indicates that the firm is making a loss.

ABC Ltd		
Income statement	2018	2017
	$000	$000
Revenue	25	22
Cost of sales	18	19
Gross profit	7	3
Fixed costs	5	4
Profits	2	(1)

Quick test

1. Explain the difference between profit and cash.
2. Explain why profits are important to businesses.
3. Describe the change in revenue between 2017 and 2018.
4. Has the business done a better or worse job of managing its cost of sales in 2018?
5. In which year did the business do a better job of managing its fixed costs?
6. In which year did the business make a loss?

The main elements of a statement of financial position

A **statement of financial position** shows the balance between the assets owned by a firm and its liabilities. It gives a snapshot of the financial health of a firm at a given point in time. This document is used by investors to establish the value of a firm.

The main classifications of assets and liabilities

- **Current assets** – these are assets owned by a business that can be turned into cash in less than a year. They might include cash, inventories and trade receivables.
- **Non-current assets** – these are assets that a business owns that cannot be turned into cash in less than a year. They might include buildings, machinery and vehicles.
- **Current liabilities** – these are debts that must be settled in the current year. They might include any trade payables and short-term borrowing debts such as an overdraft.
- **Long-term liabilities** – these are debts that are due in more than a year. They might include any mortgage debts, debentures or bank loans that a firm has taken out.

Statement of financial position

The statement of financial position below shows the balance between the assets and liabilities of a business.

- Net assets employed = current assets – current liabilities
- Capital and reserves must always be equal to the net assets employed.

Worked example

ABC Ltd	2018
Statement of financial position	$000
Non-current assets	180
Current assets	120
Current liabilities	30
Net assets employed	
Capital and reserves	90

In order to calculate the net assets employed, subtract current liabilities from current assets.

120 – 30 = 90

We can tell that this answer is correct because it is equal to the figure for capital and reserves.

> You must be able to:
> - explain the purpose of a statement of financial position
> - interpret a statement of financial position
> - consider a statement of financial position in order to make business decisions.

Revision tip

When you are practising your calculations for this part of the course, make sure that you get in the habit of showing your method. Even if you get the final answer wrong, you can gain marks for showing a formula and applying numbers correctly.

Quick test

1. What is the purpose of a statement of financial position?
2. Give two examples of current assets.
3. Explain the difference between current assets and non-current assets.
4. Explain the difference between current liabilities and long-term liabilities.

Now use the information in the table below to answer questions 5–8.

XYZ Ltd	2018	2017
Statement of financial position	$000	$000
Non-current assets	29	21
Current assets	23	25
Current liabilities	52	46
Net assets employed	29	21
Capital and reserves	29	21

5. How much working capital does this firm have in 2018?
6. How much money had to be paid back to creditors in 2017?
7. How much money was invested in the business by its owners in 2017?
8. How much extra money did the owners invest in the business in 2018?

The concept and importance of profitability

The concept and importance of profitability

Profitability refers to how efficiently a business manages its costs and maximises its revenues in order to make the highest possible profit for its owners.

A profitable business is one where the costs of production have been minimised, for example, waste has been eliminated, the best possible deals have been struck with suppliers, and costs are as low as they possibly could be.

Maximising revenue is also important to profitability. As much stock as possible must be sold for the highest possible price.

The more profitable a business is, the larger its **profit margins** are.

Profit margins

Profit margins are the difference between the cost of producing goods and services and the price for which they are sold. The larger the profit margin achieved by a firm, the more money the business makes on each sale.

The concept and importance of liquidity

Liquidity is when a business has enough current assets to be able to meet all of its current liabilities. If a business does not have enough current assets and is unable to obtain additional assets, for example by borrowing money from a bank, it will become insolvent and may need to be placed into liquidation. When a business is placed in liquidation, its non-current assets are sold in order to return as much money as possible to any creditors the firm has, in other words, to any persons or organisations to which the business owes money, for example, banks or suppliers.

You must be able to:
- outline the concept of profitability
- outline the concept of liquidity
- explain the importance of profitability and liquidity.

Revision tip

Try to think about a profit margin as being the gap between costs and income. The bigger the gap, the better the business.

Quick test

1. Explain the difference between profit and profitability.
2. Explain the meaning of the term 'profit margin'.
3. Explain the importance of liquidity to a business.

Calculating and analysing profitability ratios and liquidity ratios

Gross profit margin

Formula: Gross profit ÷ revenue × 100 = gross profit margin

This is normally expressed as a percentage. This ratio tells you how much of every dollar of revenue becomes gross profit. This is an important indication of how well a business is managing its cost of sales. If a business wants to improve its gross **profit margin**, it should try to reduce **variable costs**, for example by negotiating better deals with suppliers.

Profit margin

Formula: Profit ÷ revenue × 100 = profit margin

This ratio tells how well a business is managing its costs, particularly the **fixed costs**. It tells you how much of each dollar of revenue becomes profit. If a business wants to improve its profit margin, it could reduce its fixed costs, for example by relocating to cheaper premises.

Return on Capital Employed (ROCE)

Formula: Profit ÷ capital employed × 100 = ROCE

This ratio tells the owners of a business how efficiently its investment is performing. It tells them how much money the business is making with the money that has been invested in it. The higher the ROCE percentage, the more money the firm is making with its resources each year.

Current ratio

Formula: Current assets ÷ current liabilities = current ratio

If this ratio is 1, this means that for every dollar of debts that are due this year, the business has one dollar of liquid assets. This means that the business would be able to pay all of its debts if they were all called in at once.

Ideally, this figure should be between 0.8 and 1.2. If it is too low, for example, below 0.8, this suggests that the firm has **liquidity** problems and might struggle to pay its debts. If the ratio is too high, for example, above 1.2, this suggests that the firm is using money inefficiently.

You must be able to:
- calculate a range of profitability and liquidity ratios
- interpret the results of ratio calculations
- consider the performance of a range of firms using ratio calculations.

 Revision tip

Try calculating these ratios based on the income statement and statement of financial position for ABC Ltd and XYZ Ltd from earlier in this chapter. How would you judge the performance of these firms based on your results?

Acid test ratio

Formula: (Current assets – stock) ÷ current liabilities

This ratio addresses a problem with the current ratio. Current assets include stock, but a business that holds a lot of stock might not be able to convert it into **cash** immediately if it suddenly had to settle all of its debts. This ratio tells you how much of a firm's current liabilities could be settled without selling any stock.

Quick test

1. How do profit margins help managers make decisions?
2. Why is ROCE an important measure to potential investors?
3. Why is the acid test ratio more useful to managers than the current ratio?

Why and how accounts are used

Needs of different users of accounts and ratio analysis

- Managers – they can use accounts and ratios to make comparisons with other, similar firms. Calculating ratios allows them to see if their firm is performing as well as its competitors. Calculating ratios enables them to make a relatively objective comparison, controlling for differences in the size of the firms.
- Shareholders and investors – they might want to look at a **statement of financial position** in order to check the value of a firm before they take a risk by investing their money. They may also want to examine ratios to see how efficiently the firm is being managed.
- Competitors – they might want to examine a company's accounts to see how well they perform compared to their own business. The process of comparing the performance of one firm with that of another is called **benchmarking**.

How users of accounts and ratio results might use information to help make decisions

An analysis of the accounts of a business might be used to make a number of decisions:

- **Whether to lend to the business** – if a business already has high levels of current or fixed liabilities, banks might not be willing to lend money to the firm. Alternatively, if the firm has a low current ratio or acid test ratio, this might discourage potential lenders because the firm might struggle to pay back the debt if problems were to arise.
- **Whether to invest in the business** – if a business has a large number of assets or high revenues and low costs, this might make it an attractive target for investors.

Revision tip

When you evaluate a set of accounts, try to imagine the audience that you are presenting your findings to – what are they interested in? Why?

Quick test

1. Explain why two different groups of stakeholders might want to review the accounts of a business.
2. Discuss one limitation of carrying out ratio analysis.

1 Lend 2u is a social enterprise which provides small loans to people who are struggling to manage to make their wages last until the end of the month. The business is based in a small town in country E where there are high levels of unemployment. The business needs large amounts of cash each day as working capital.

Lend 2u relies on grants from the government for much of its funding but it also receives money from donations and as interest on the repayments of loans. Sometimes the business needs extra cash during busy months. For this, it relies on an overdraft facility at its own bank. The company is investing in new equipment. The trustees of the business are using a cashflow forecast to plan the best time to make this investment.

Lend 2u		
Income statement	2018	2017
	$000	$000
Revenue	95	64
Cost of sales	45	60
Gross profit	A	B
Fixed costs	12	9
Profits	C	D

a) Define the term 'short term finance'.   [2

b) Define the term 'working capital'.   [2

c) Outline the benefits of using a cashflow forecast to decide when to invest in new equipment.   [4

d) Explain two drawbacks of using an overdraft as a source of finance.   [6

e) Calculate the gross and net profits made by Lend 2u in 2017 (B and D) and 2018 (A and C).

   Do you think that retained profit is an appropriate source of finance for this business? Justify your answer.   [6

2 Not Very Ltd is a consultancy business that specialises in helping small companies set up their ICT infrastructure. The balance sheet for the business for 2017 and 2018 is shown below.

Not Very Ltd	2018	2017
Statement of financial position	$000	$000
Non-current assets	90	87
Current assets	56	53
Current liabilities	49	47
Net assets employed	97	93
Capital and reserves	97	93

The business currently allows customers up to 60 days to pay their bills.

a) Define the term 'statement of financial position'. [2]

b) Define the term 'current asset'. [2]

c) Calculate the current ratio for 2017 and 2018.

Outline the significance of the change in the ratio. [4]

d) Explain two reasons why the acid test ratio might a most useful way to measure the liquidity of the business. [6]

e) The finance manager of the business is considering two options:

 – reducing the amount of stock that the business holds

 – encouraging customers to pay their bills in less than 60 days

 Which is the most appropriate method of improving the management of working capital at Not Very Ltd? [6]

Business cycle

Main stages of the business cycle

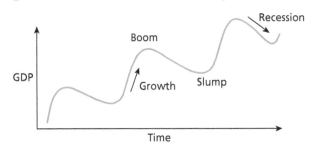

- **Growth** – this is when the **economy** is expanding. **Gross Domestic Product (GDP)** is growing and therefore standards of living are likely to be rising.
- **Boom** – this is when economic growth peaks and GDP reaches its highest point of the economic cycle. Standards of living are likely to be high, but so is **inflation**, which will begin to put pressure on the spending power of people unless their employers increase their incomes.
- **Recession** – This is when an economy goes through two or more consecutive quarters of negative growth. This is a period of time when incomes are falling throughout the economy, unemployment is likely to be rising, and standards of living are likely to be falling.
- **Slump** – This is when the economy reaches the lowest level of economic growth and is the lowest point of a recession. This is when unemployment will be highest and standards of living will be lowest. Governments are likely to try techniques such as lowering interest rates to try to increase the amount of **consumer spending** in the economy and thus restart economic growth.

Impact on businesses of changes in employment levels

High unemployment can be good for firms that want to hire workers. This is because more people will apply for every job vacancy and firms might be able to pay them lower wages. On the other hand, consumer demand will be lower because fewer people will be working and therefore less money will be spent, especially on luxury goods.

Impact on businesses of changes in Inflation

Inflation is the rate at which prices are increasing. When the economy is performing well and GDP is growing, inflation is likely to be high. This can be both good and bad for firms. Firms will earn more revenue because of rising prices but they might make lower profits because inflation also causes the costs of **raw materials** to increase.

Impact on businesses of changes in GDP

When GDP grows, consumer confidence increases and people are willing to spend more money, particularly on luxury goods. More people will be in work, which might make it harder to recruit staff.

How government control over the economy affects business activity and how businesses may respond

Identify government economic objectives

The economic **objectives** that governments set will depend on which stage of the **business cycle** the **economy** has reached. For example, when an economy is in a slump, increasing **GDP** and reducing unemployment might be especially important. When an economy is in a **boom**, the government might find it more important to focus on controlling **inflation**.

- **Increasing GDP** – rising GDP is a sign that an economy is performing well and that the country is becoming increasingly prosperous. Governments will aim to increase GDP because this will also mean that as people get richer, they will pay more taxes, which governments can spend on their political priorities.
- **Achieving full employment** – governments aim to keep unemployment as low as possible. This means that more people have a higher standard of living and they are likely to be happier. Governments might try to achieve this by paying **subsidies** to firms that hire more staff. This can benefit businesses by reducing their costs if they hire people such as the long-term unemployed.
- **Balance of trade** – governments will aim to achieve an overall balance between the quantity of goods exported to other countries and the quantity of goods imported into their country. It is important to balance the needs of the public, who might like cheap goods from overseas, and businesses that might want to sell their products overseas to other markets.
- **Low Inflation** – governments want to maintain inflation at a low level. This is because high levels of inflation mean that people's standard of living declines as their money loses its purchasing power. High inflation also increases the price of goods, making them less attractive to foreign firms that might want to buy goods from local exporters.

Impact of changes in taxes

When taxes increase, this can have a number of effects:

If income taxes rise, consumers might spend less money. This will reduce GDP but it will also reduce inflation. If a government does increase taxes, it will have more money to spend on projects such as building roads and schools.

If Value Added Taxes (VAT) rise, the price of goods and services will increase, leading to inflation. This will lead to a lower standard of living for families, making more people unhappy. It will cause the revenue earned by firms to increase. However, this will not lead to higher profits because firms will have to pay more money to the government in VAT.

Impact of changes in government spending

Changes in government spending can have a number of different effects, depending on the priorities of the government.

- Governments might invest in **infrastructure** such as roads or education. This could benefit businesses. For example, investment in education could lead to a workforce with more skills, enabling them to be more productive workers. Investment in roads would mean that businesses could function more effectively, for example through deliveries reaching their destinations sooner.
- Governments might choose to provide additional **subsidies** to firms. This would reduce the risks of investing in new markets or it might increase the potential **profitability** of other markets, which would act as an incentive for firms to invest.
- Governments might save money by reducing the amount of money they spend on **benefits**. This would increase levels of poverty, leading to fewer customers for some businesses. However, it might mean that more people are looking for work, leading to more choice when hiring staff.

Impact of changes in interest rates

Increases in interest rates will affect savers and borrowers.

- Savers will spend less money and save more if interest rates go up. This will mean that businesses will have lower revenues as people put more of their income into savings accounts such as ISAs.
- Borrowers will find that the cost of repaying their debts will increase. This is because interest rates represent the cost of borrowing. If businesses have borrowed money to fund **working capital** or expansion, this will increase their costs and reduce profits.

Quick test

1. What are the main objectives of government policy?
2. What does the term GDP mean?
3. Why do governments want to achieve a low level of unemployment?
4. Why is a balance of imports and exports important to governments?
5. What is inflation?
6. How does inflation affect businesses?
7. Why do governments set taxes?
8. Name two types of tax.
9. How do increases in taxes affect businesses?
10. How will an increase in interest rates affect consumers?

Environmental and ethical issues

Chapter 6
External
influences on
business
activity

Environmental concerns and ethical issues as both opportunities and constraints for businesses

How business activity can impact on the environment

Business activity can impact on the environment in a number of ways. Factories might emit pollutants that contribute to global warming. Some companies have caused deforestation in areas such as the Amazon rainforest, which not only increases global warming but also causes the loss of habitats and the extinction of species of animals and plants.

The concept of externalities

Business activity has a number of possible external cost benefits that are felt by the wider community, not the business; these are called **externalities**. When business decisions have a negative impact on society, for example, pollution, this is an instance of a **negative externality**. When a business has a positive effect on society, for example, redeveloping polluted industrial land to build a new office complex, this is an instance of a **positive externality**.

Sustainable development

Business activity can contribute to sustainable development by investing in facilities and creating jobs in developing countries. As more people enter the workforce, this leads to higher tax revenues allowing more government investment into the local economy, creating more jobs, and so the business cycle continues.

How and why business might respond to environmental pressures and opportunities

Businesses can respond to environmental pressures by improving their production processes in order to reduce pollution. However, this will depend on the priorities of the company. If the main priority of the company is profit, reducing costs will be considered to be more important than protecting the environment.

Pressure groups try to influence the decisions of businesses. This can be through protests and campaigns. Unless the activities of pressure groups damages the public image of a firm, or reduces the level of profit made by a firm, it is unlikely that they will have a major impact.

> **You must be able to:**
> - outline a range of environmental and ethical issues that can affect businesses
> - explain the impact of different ethical and environmental issues on a range of businesses.

> **Revision tip**
>
> Can you think of any recent examples of businesses that have acted ethically or unethically? Have there been any scandals caused by a big firm creating large externalities?

Environmental and ethical issues

The role of legal controls over business activity affecting the environment

Many governments set rules to ensure that businesses behave well. One example of this is pollution controls. This may mean that businesses have to monitor the emission of fumes from their factories or dispose of waste materials in an environmentally friendly way. This type of legislation will lead to higher costs for businesses. Some firms lobby governments to reduce the number of these laws.

Ethical issues a business might face: the conflict between profits and ethics

Most businesses exist in order to make a profit for their shareholders. While they may view **ethics** as important, the main priority of managers and company directors is to maximise the returns made for shareholders.

Given that managers have an obligation to maximise shareholder value, this often means that ethical concerns come second to profits.

How businesses might react and respond to ethical issues

Businesses might respond to ethical issues, for example, using child labour, by running public relations campaigns to minimise the damage to their reputations and to emphasise positive ways in which they contribute to society.

Other firms might respond by reviewing their business practices to ensure that they are meeting ethical standards.

Quick test

1. List five ethical issues that might affect a business.
2. Explain two environmental issues that might affect a business.
3. Explain why managers might struggle to balance ethics and profits.

The importance of globalisation

The concept of globalisation and the reasons for it

Globalisation means that businesses are increasingly trading across international borders, and that the same brands can be seen in shops all around the world. It is becoming simpler for firms to operate globally as the world becomes more interconnected. Improved transport links means that products can travel large distances more quickly and at a lower cost than ever before.

Communication technologies such as the internet enable firms to send consistent marketing messages across the world. Global brands such as McDonald's and Starbucks are recognised wherever they operate.

Opportunities and threats of globalisation for businesses

Opportunities	Threats
• Businesses can increase profits by moving production to low-cost economies. • Huge numbers of customers can be targeted by trading with large numbers of companies. • Better transportation makes it more economical to export goods to other countries. • Operating in many countries allows businesses to gain larger economies of scale.	• Global businesses can be seen as greedy as they often operate in countries with the lowest taxes to maximise their profits. • Global businesses can be seen as exploitative because they may take advantage of less stringent labour and pollution regulations in developing countries.

> **Revision tip**

Globalisation is all around you. Next time you go shopping, look to see where your food comes from. How much choice would you lose if you couldn't buy from global markets? How would this impact your quality of life?

Why governments might introduce import tariffs and import quotas

- An **import tariff** is a tax that is applied on goods imported into a country.
- A **quota** is a limit placed on the number of certain goods that can be brought into a specific country.

Governments will use these forms of **protectionism** to protect **domestic industry** from foreign competitors.

Quick test

1. What does the term 'globalisation' mean?
2. Name three global businesses.
3. Outline two benefits of globalisation for consumers.
4. Outline two drawbacks of globalisation for governments.

Business and the international economy

Reasons for the importance and growth of multinational companies

Benefits to a business of becoming a multinational and the impact on its stakeholders

A multinational company (MNC) can locate its operations in countries where laws, regulations and taxes allow it to make the highest possible profits.

It is also possible for a company that operates as an MNC to access a wider pool of talent when they recruit staff.

Most important of all, a business that operates as an MNC can access a significantly greater number of potential customers, giving it an opportunity to make much higher profits than might otherwise have been possible.

Potential benefits to a country and/or economy where an MNC is located

- Jobs – many local people will need to be employed in a range of roles, including manufacturing, **customer service** and management.
- Exports – goods produced by the MNC may be exported to other markets, increasing the **GDP** of a country.
  Increased choice – the MNC is likely to produce goods and services for the local market, offering **consumers** a wider range of products to choose from.
  Investment – when an MNC opens new premises, it will often invest money in **infrastructure**, providing, for example, better roads.

Potential drawbacks to a country and/or economy where an MNC is located

Reduced sales for local businesses – large global brands might be more appealing to local consumers, thereby reducing the revenue earned by local companies. This might lead to smaller local firms going out of business as a result of the **competition**.

Repatriation of profits – profits made by an MNC are sent back to another country. This means that money is being drained from the economy where the MNC is located.

You must be able to:
- outline why businesses become multinational companies
- explain the benefits and drawbacks to countries of investment by multinational companies
- explain the impact of exchange rates on international trade.

The impact of exchange rate changes

An **exchange rate** is the value of one country's currency in terms of another country's currency.

Depreciation and appreciation of an exchange rate

When an exchange rate **depreciates**, your currency is worth less compared to other currencies. This means that you can buy fewer goods from abroad, but your exports are cheaper and so might sell in greater numbers. The opposite is true of a currency **appreciation**.

If the pound appreciates (becomes worth more in other currencies), it will be cheaper to import goods into the UK but more expensive to export goods abroad. The same rule holds true for other currencies.

How exchange rate changes can affect businesses as importers and exporters of products

- Prices – when an **exchange rate** appreciates, it might be cheaper to make certain goods because imported **raw materials** become cheaper. This might allow firms to reduce their prices.
- Competitiveness – when an exchange rate appreciates, this makes exporters less competitive because it means their goods and services will be more expensive in other countries. However, the reduction in the cost of imports will increase the amount of **competition** for domestic suppliers.
- Profitability – an exchange rate appreciation will lead to an increase in the profitability of firms that import their raw materials because those costs will be lower. But this might be balanced by the need to cut prices to compete with cheaper imported goods.

Revision tip

Do you know the current exchange rates for the pound? The dollar? The euro?

How will these rates affect the businesses that you rely on?

Revision tip

The acronym SPICED is useful for remembering the impact of a currency appreciation. It stands for: Strong Pound Imports Cheap Exports Dear.

Quick test

1. Define the term 'exchange rate'.
2. What happens when the exchange rate of a currency appreciates?
3. How will the profitability of exporters be affected by an appreciation in exchange rates?

Exam-style practice questions

1 The main town Chamber of Commerce provides advice and support to businesses to help improve their performance. The organisation publishes reports on the impact of economic factors such as the business cycle and inflation.

The Chamber of Commerce lobbies the government on behalf of its members to ensure that government policies influence the economy in a way that helps businesses. The Chamber of Commerce helps its members to understand the impact of taxes and provides advice on the impact of changes on interest rates.

a) Define 'business cycle'. [2]

b) Define 'inflation'. [2]

c) Outline methods that the government might use to influence the economy in order to help businesses. [4]

d) Explain two ways that an increase in taxes might impact on the businesses that the Chamber of Commerce represents. [6]

e) Consider the impact of interest rates on an economy. An increase in interest rates will affect:

   – individuals and firms which are saving money

   – individuals and firms which are borrowing money

   Which of these groups will an increase in interest rates have a larger impact on?
   Justify your answer. [6]

2 Clean Corporation manufactures chemicals used in the cleaning of factories. These substances are highly toxic and require specialist equipment to safely make, store and distribute them. The staff involved in the production of these chemicals must be highly skilled.

Clean Corporation have invested a large amount of money developing production facilities in country F, including a substantial investment in the training and education of workers. The company has focused on the environmental standards of its factory, taking every possible step to limit its impact on the environment including investment in the latest technology and having strict procedures for handling chemicals. The business has made smaller profits as a result of these measures.

The business has taken advantage of the increasing tendency towards globalisation and bases its head office in country G where taxes on profits are low. The government of country F feels that Clean Corporation has a number of negative effects on its population, including high levels of cancer in people living near the factories, low wages and long hours of work for employees, and a decrease in river levels caused by the factory draining rivers for its production processes.

a) Explain four benefits of sustainable development. [8]

b) Explain why the following three factors lead to a conflict between ethics and profit:

- investment in new technology

- strict rules and procedures

- high levels of training and education for staff

Which of these factors causes the greatest conflict? Justify your answer. [12]

c) Explain four benefits of globalisation. [8]

d) Explain how the following three factors are negative externalities of Clean Corporation's production process:

- drawing water from rivers to use in production

- high rates of cancer near the factory

- low wages and long hours for employees.

Which of these factors is the greatest externality? Justify your answer. [12]

Chapter 1 Understanding business activity

Business activity: Quick test (page 7)
1. Needs and wants are infinite but resources are limited so there will never be enough to satisfy everyone's needs and wants.
2. Possible answers:
Petrol – there is only a limited amount of oil in the world.
Potatoes – farmers plant only a certain amount of each crop every year.
Haircuts – a hairdresser can only serve a limited number of customers every day.
Cars – factories have a limited capacity to make cars.
Meals in restaurants – there is a limited number of tables in each restaurant.
3. a) A business owner might have to choose between an advertising campaign and buying more stock.
   b) A consumer might have to choose between buying a product or a service.
4. Possible answers:
Efficiency – producing a large amount of a specific product is likely to be more efficient because workers will repeatedly perform the same tasks and therefore get very good at them.
Competition – a specific niche in the market may be more profitable than others, making it worth while focusing on that one area.
5. Possible answers:
By branding – placing a recognised brand on products will make people more willing to pay higher prices if they value that specific brand.
By combining raw materials into a finished product which meets customers' needs.
By processing raw materials into a usable form, for example, making petrol and diesel from crude oil.

Classification of business: Quick test (page 9)
1. Primary industry – businesses that extract raw materials from the ground or the sea.
Secondary industry – businesses that transform raw materials into finished goods.
Tertiary industry – businesses that provide services to consumers.
Shell Oil Company has oil rigs that extract oil from under the sea (primary), oil refineries where crude oil is turned into petrol, diesel and oil (secondary), and petrol stations that sell fuel to drivers (tertiary).
Possible answers: higher levels of education in developed economies, meaning that workers will be more skilled; higher average income in developed economies, meaning that consumers can buy more goods and services; lower wages in developing economies, meaning that production costs will be lower.
Possible answers:
Many primary services have invested money and other resources into developing tertiary industry, which has higher added value, such as banking and financial services.
Developed economies might have controls on pollution and development of land in rural areas that make activities such as mining impractical.
Public sector – organisations owned and controlled by government agencies.

Private sector – organisations owned by private individuals or businesses.
6. Possible answers: to develop emerging technologies, for example, renewable energy, that might not be profitable for the private sector; to provide services that might not be provided by the private sector, for example, education, that are beneficial to society.

Enterprise and entrepreneurship: Quick test (page 11)
1. Possible answers: resilience; creativity; determination; charisma.
2. Cashflow forecast – a prediction of how much money will come into and go out of a business.
Cost and revenue forecasts – how much the business is likely to spend on raw materials and how much it plans to charge customers.
Aims and objectives – goals of the company.
Marketing mix – how the business will sell its goods to the public.
Organisational chart – the structure of the business and what kind of roles and responsibilities staff will hold.
3. Possible answers: to secure funding from a bank; so that employees know what the business aims to achieve; so that the owner can monitor progress against their initial plans; so that the business has a clear sense of direction.
4. Possible answers: by providing grants or low-interest loans; by reducing tax rates for small firms; by removing laws that restrict business activities.
5. Possible answers:
To reduce unemployment so that people starting firms do not need to claim social security payments and so that there is a chance their firms may grow to a point where they employ people themselves; to increase GDP – more businesses mean more economic activity, which means more national income.

Business growth and size: Quick test (page 14)
1. Possible answers: opening new stores, mergers, acquisitions, expanding into a new market.
2. Internal growth is when a business extends the reach of its existing operations rather than buying another company in order to grow larger.
3. Possible answers: poor management; economic conditions; changes in competition.
4. Possible answers: new businesses are not likely to have developed relationships with their customers or have loyalty from customers. They face intense competition from other new market entrants.

Business organisations: Quick test (page 17)
1. Possible answers: total control of the business; no paperwork needed to start up; can keep all the profits.
2. Possible answers: possibility of disagreements; need to share profits between partners; partners are liable for debts incurred by one another.
3. It is a business such as a sole trader or a partnership that is not owned by shareholders.
4. Possible answers: they benefit from limited liability so there is less risk of losing their personal possessions if the business fails. There is extra scope to raise capital for expansion by selling.
5. They have unlimited liability and therefore their personal possessions can be seized by creditors if they cannot pay business debts.
6. Possible answers: how much risk people are willing to accept; how many people will own the business; how much

capital needs to be raised; for example, is there a need to sell shares?

7. Possible answers: private sector firms exist to make profits for their owners while public sector firms tend to exist to provide a service to the public. Public sector firms are owned by the state while private sector firms are owned by individuals or companies.

Business and stakeholder objectives: Quick test (page 19)

1. A goal that is set by the managers of a business, and that they intend to achieve in a certain period of time.
2. So that there is a clear focus for the activities of staff and managers, and to make sure that resources are used efficiently.
3. Possible answers: to gain market share; maximise profits; survival; business growth; minimising costs; increase revenue.
4. A person or group who have an interest in or are affected by the activities of a business.
5. Possible answers: customers; pressure groups; suppliers; local residents; competitors.

Exam-style practice questions (pages 20–21)

1. a) The things that are essential to the survival of an individual [1] such as food and shelter [1]. **[2 marks]**
    b) When a business is owned by one person [1] who has unlimited liability [1]. **[2 marks]**
    c) The government might provide grants [1] which would allow investment in new equipment [1] allowing the business to serve more customers [1] and therefore increasing potential revenue [1]. **[4 marks]**
    d) The growth of the business could be measured in terms of how much revenue is earned [1] if this increases from month to month [1] then the business can be said to be growing [1]. Alternatively, the business could count how many play-centres it operates [1]. If the business opens a new centre [1] then it will be bigger because it can serve more customers [1]. **[6 marks]**
    e) Risk-taking is important because no business is guaranteed to be a success [1] and so therefore entrepreneurs must be willing to face the risk of losing some or all of the money that they invest [1] if the business fails [1].
        Another important attribute is resilience [1]; an entrepreneur might make a lot of mistakes while they are developing their business idea [1] but they would need to make sure that they are able to keep on going until they get the idea right [1]. **[6 marks]**

2. a) A private limited company has limited liability [1] meaning that Chad's personal possessions will be safe [1] in the event of business failure [1] as creditors will only be able to seize business assets [1].
        Another reason to become a private limited company would be because shares in a private limited company can only be sold with the agreement of other shareholders [1] which would mean that if Chad sold shares in his business to raise capital [1] he would have greater security [1] and that the ownership of the business could not change without his agreement [1]. **[8 marks]**
    b) Help and support is important to running the business as a franchise because the franchisor is likely to have a great deal of expertise in running that type of business [1] which means that Chad can ask questions about technical aspects of the business [1] such as cooking the food [1] in order to ensure that the business operates to the same standard as other franchises [1]. Centralised promotional campaigns mean that the money that Chad pays as his franchise fee will contribute towards promotional costs [1] meaning that the

franchisor is able to promote the business on a national or regional scale [1] gaining economies of scale for purchasing larger amounts of advertising from media channels [1] and therefore gaining greater reach with promotional material than Chad could gain advertising on his own [1].
    A franchisee has limited freedom to make decisions [1] because they have to abide by rules set by the franchisor [1] such as where to buy raw materials / how to carry out promotional activity [1] even if Chad believes his own ideas might improve the business [1]. **[12 marks]**
    c) Two possible objectives for Chad's business might be:
        1) Increase the number of customers visiting the restaurant each week by ten per cent [1]. This is a target that the business owner hopes to achieve [1] which would contribute to an increase in revenue [1] by increasing the number of people visiting the restaurant, many of whom might spend money [1].
        2) Increase the amount of money that each customer spends by 20 per cent each visit [1]. By focusing on selling more items to each customer [1] Chad could potentially increase his profits [1] by focusing on upselling to customers [1]. **[8 mark**
    d) The impact of The Great Burger Company on pressure groups might be that they choose to increase their number of protests [1] because they object to the slaughter of animals for use in food [1] and want to try and discourage the public from visiting branches of The Great Burger Company [1].
        An impact on staff is that they might be frightened of coming to work when pressure groups are protesting [1] because they find the protestors intimidating [1]. However, they also benefit from an income [1].
        An impact on customers might be that they are reluctant to go to The Great Burger Company [1] if it is difficult to get into the branch [1] and choose to eat at a competitor's instead [1].
        The group that this has the biggest impact on is likely to be the staff as they have no choice about going to the restaurant [1] because they have to meet the terms of their contracts [1] and therefore cannot be deterred by protestors [1]. **[12 mark**
    e) Primary industry is extracting raw materials from the ground [1], this might mean farming animals / growing potatoes [1]; this is important to Chad because these items are his raw materials [1]. Secondary industry is the processing of raw materials [1], which might mean turning cows into burgers [1], which matters to The Great Burger Company because these are their raw materials [1]. Tertiary industry matters to The Great Burger Company because this is the market that they compete in [1] – they provide services such as cooking and serving food to customers [1]. **[8 mark**
    f) The Great Burger Company should choose to increase the price of chips because this will lower demand [1], reducing the pressure on them to get hold of stock [1]; but it will also give them more revenue [1] with which to buy the more expensive raw materials [1], which is a better option than buying lower quality products because otherwise customers may not be satisfied [1] as the chips they buy would be of a lower standard than usual [1], leading them to have a lower opinion of The Great Burger Company [1] and thus making them less likely to go there again [1]. **[8 mark**

Chapter 2 People in business

Motivating employees: Quick test (page 23)
1. The willingness to work and complete tasks.
2. Maslow's hierarchy; Herzberg's two-factor theory; Taylor's scientific management.
3. Financial incentives relate to extrinsic rewards such as money, while non-financial rewards relate to intrinsic rewards such as having a more satisfying job.

Draw, interpret and understand simple organisational charts: Quick test (page 25)
1. Answers will vary depending on the case studies used during the course but should include relevant levels and job titles, and should have 'span of control' and 'chain of command' annotated on the sketch.
2. 'Chain of command' is a path from an employee at the bottom of the hierarchy to the overall leader of the business at the top. 'Span of control' is the group of workers that report to a specific manager or supervisor.
3. Managers co-ordinate resources and control the day-to-day activities of the business to ensure that targets are met and resources are used efficiently.

Leadership styles: Quick test (page 27)
1. Possible answers: Autocratic – gives workers orders and expects them to obey;
Democratic – takes time to find out and consider the views of workers before taking decisions.
2. Autocratic leadership might be best as the business will be in a crisis and will need to make quick decisions to resolve the problems that are potentially going to lead to bankruptcy. Taking the time to have a democratic approach would take too much time and the business needs to act quickly in order to survive.
3. A group that represents the interests of workers in a particular industry.
4. Possible answers:
Collective bargaining leads to higher wages for employees.
There is representation for workers who are involved in disciplinary meetings or who have other problems.

Recruitment and selection methods: Quick test (page 29)
1. Decide what kind of worker you need.
Write a job description so that you know what kind of work they will do.
Write a person specification so that you know what kind of person you want to hire.
Produce a job advert based on the person specification and job description.
Shortlist applicants against the person specification.
Interview applicants on the shortlist.
Appoint the best interviewee.
2. The manager will already know the business and the staff. It will not be necessary for them to take time to familiarise themselves with the business. They can get started right away.
3. Full-time workers will spend more time at their job and will be more experienced at completing tasks more quickly. They may feel more committed to the employer because they spend more time at work.

The importance of training and the methods of training: Quick test (page 31)
1. Induction; on-the-job; off-the-job.
2. To equip workers with new skills; to make business practices more efficient; to bring new ideas into the business.
3. To save money; to remain competitive; in response to new technology.

4. a) The firm will have lower costs and therefore might be in a better position to survive problems such as a recession.
b) Employees will be demotivated because they might be worried about their own job security and unhappy to see friends and colleagues leaving.

Legal controls over employment issues and their impact on employers and employees: Quick test (page 32)
1. Possible answers: minimum wage; health and safety; discrimination; contracts; unfair dismissal.
2. Possible answer:
The recruitment process would have to give a fair opportunity to people regardless of race, religion, gender, sexuality or disability so as not to discriminate.
The employee would need to be given a contract once hired.
3. Possible answers:
Health and safety – workers would need to be given a workplace that does not pose a risk of injury.
Minimum wage – workers would need to be paid at least the minimum legally required amount, increasing average unit costs.

Why effective communication is important and the methods used to achieve it: Quick test (page 34)
1. To ensure that staff understand how to do their jobs properly; to ensure that customers and consumers understand what they are being offered.
2. Emails; meetings; phone calls.
3. Physical barriers – reorganising office space; cultural barriers – changing working practices and retraining staff.
4. Staff will not be well co-ordinated; they will not know what to do or when to do it, leading to missed targets and poorly used resources.
Customers will not understand what the business is offering them and therefore might not spend their money there.

Exam-style practice questions (pages 35–36)
1. a) Motivation is the desire to do something [1] which is an internal psychological force [1]. **[2 marks]**
b) Non-financial motivation is when factors such as job enrichment [1] are used to create the desire to do something in workers [1]. **[2 marks]**
c) The manager looks after eight members of staff meaning a wide span of control [1]; this might mean that it's harder to supervise each worker [1], meaning that they are less inclined to work [1] because they feel nobody is paying attention to them [1]. **[4 marks]**
d) The first factor would be the physiological needs of the staff [1] such as giving them access to basic facilities such as bathrooms [1] because if these basic needs are not met [1] then the workers will not be able to progress further up the hierarchy [1].
Another factor might be love and belonging needs [1]: workers will benefit from working in groups with colleagues [1]. **[6 marks]**
e) Motivated workers will be more productive [1] meaning that they are able to generate more revenue for the business [1] at a lower cost [1].
But on the other hand, it might be more important to control the use of resources [1] which would also mean that costs are lower [1] and therefore profits are higher [1]. **[6 marks]**
2. a) Autocratic leadership is when the boss gives orders to staff [1]; this means that things will get done faster [1] because there is no need to wait for discussions about what workers want to do [1] meaning the business can respond more quickly to changes in the environment [1].
Another benefit is that there will be clarity about who is in charge [1] the leader will not delegate

decision-making to anyone [1] and therefore there will be no uncertainty amongst workers about what to do [1] as they can simply ask the boss if they are unsure [1].
[8 marks]

b) Collective bargaining is when workers negotiate with managers as a group [1] giving them more power to influence decisions [1] and therefore increasing the chances of favourable decisions such as a pay rise [1]. Protection of rights comes from the work that unions do to educate workers about their rights [1] and to represent them in discussions with management [1] and providing people who are experts on the rights of workers to help make discussions run smoothly [1]. Industrial action is when workers take action to protest their treatment by managers [1] such as going on strike or imposing a "work to rule" [1] this can influence decisions made by managers in favour of workers [1]. The most important factor is collective bargaining because this gives workers one voice [1] and they are represented by expert union negotiators [1] who can get them better deals than the workers could expect if they negotiated alone [1]. **[12 marks]**

c) Internal recruitment is when people that already work at a business get appointed to new roles in the company [1] this can be beneficial to the business because it is cheaper than external recruitment [1] because, for example, they will not need to advertise vacancies in newspapers [1] and can inform workers with a note on a staffroom noticeboard [1]. Another benefit could be that the workers hired will already know the business well [1] reducing the amount of time and money needed to train them [1] and allowing them to get started in their new job right away [1] as they already know all of the staff and procedures that they need to know about [1]. **[8 marks]**

d) • Staff might take industrial action [1] which would lead to negative publicity [1].
• Remaining staff may feel a lack of job security [1] leading to a loss in motivation [1].
• Making staff redundant will mean that skilled workers will be lost [1] potentially leading to a loss in productivity [1].
• The costs to the business will be reduced [1] making the remaining, smaller operation more productive [1].
[8 marks]

e) If the managing director chose the workers that get made redundant himself he could remove staff with skills that are no longer needed [1] while retaining talented staff [1] that might be useful to him in the future [1] who would be able to make a contribution to the company's future plans [1]. But this might make staff unhappy / demotivated [1] leading to a reduction in productivity [1] because people are frightened about their futures and whether they will be next to be made redundant [1]. On the other hand, if he allows the staff to take voluntary redundancy this would allow people that are not happy in their jobs to leave [1] or people that are ready to retire anyway [1] and they might even feel positive about leaving [1] leading to a better atmosphere in the workplace [1] but overall, he should choose the workers that he makes redundant himself so that the staff that go are the ones that are least useful to the business [1]. **[12 marks]**

Chapter 3 Marketing

Marketing, competition and the consumer:
Quick test (page 38)
1. It is important so that customers are satisfied with their experience and consequently come back to make repeat purchases.

2. Customer loyalty is when customers choose a business over that of competitors because they prefer the goods and services it offers.
3. It is important in order to understand their needs better so that they can be targeted with additional goods and services, increasing the profitability of the business.
4. Mass markets aim standardised products at the largest possible number of people, while niche markets focus on things that satisfy smaller numbers of people with specific needs.

Market changes: Quick test (page 40)
1. Technologies might make a product obsolete. Customers' tastes and preferences might change over time as fashions change.
2. New technologies might make it cheaper to make goods, lowering prices and therefore giving items broader appeal. Technology might lead to whole new products or classes of products being developed.
3. Customers expect to be able to access a wider range of goods and services.
They increasingly shop online. They expect to access goods and services 24 hours a day.
4. Demographically, geographically, psychographically.
5. They segment it in order to target resources efficiently at the specific groups of customers that are most likely to buy their goods/services.

The role of market research and methods used:
Quick test (page 42)
1. Primary, secondary.
2. Possible answers: survey – sending out a questionnaire to a sample group (people who are representative of the target market); focus group – getting a group of people to discuss a product or service in order to observe their responses and gather their opinions.
3. So that the sample properly represents the target market, allowing the collection of data which is valid and reliable.
4. Possible answers: the skills of the researcher; the design of the questions; the sampling method used; the age of the secondary data collected.

Presentation and use of market research results:
Quick test (page 44)
1. E
2. That revenue increases as spending on advertising increases
3. Revenue is decreasing over time.

Marketing mix: product: Quick test (page 46)
1. The stages that a product goes through from when it is first developed to when it is withdrawn from the market.
2. Introduction, growth, maturity, decline and (on occasions) extension strategy.
3. Maturity and decline.
4. Decline.

Marketing mix: price: Quick test (page 48)
1. Possible answers: cost-plus; promotional pricing; penetration pricing; price skimming.
2. Possible answers: competition; demand; intended positioning
3. Price elasticity states how sensitive customers are to change in price. If a product is price inelastic, increases in price won't reduce revenue. If a product is price elastic, reducing prices is likely to increase sales revenue and potentially increase profits.

Marketing mix: place: Quick test (page 50)
1. The way that a business gets goods and services to its market
2. In order to increase the amount of profit made on each sale
3. Possible answers: the brand image of the business; the level of profit required; whether they are entering a domestic or an international market; the type of customer being targeted.

Marketing mix: promotion: Quick test (page 51)

1. Promotion is the name given to activities used to communicate with customers and consumers, normally with the aim of stimulating demand.
2. Advertising involves paying to place a message to customers in a media channel such as a newspaper or on the radio. Sales promotion involves the reduction of prices or offering customers a free gift/competition to encourage them to buy.
3. The purpose of promotion is to increase the number and value of sales, but if the promotional activity costs more than it raises in additional revenue then it will lead to the business making a loss.

Technology and the marketing mix: Quick test (page 52)

1. Product, price, place, promotion.
2. Advertising – paying for space in media channels to tell consumers about products/services;
   sponsorship – paying to place a brand name on other products/services, for example, football shirts;
   special offer pricing – using discounts to encourage people to buy goods.
3. Technology might change the type of products you are competing against.
   It might offer new ways to communicate with the public.
   It might allow a reduction in the price of goods due to cheaper production.
   It might lead to new distribution channels opening up.

Recommend and justify marketing strategies appropriate to a given situation: Quick test (page 53)

. Possible answer (one of the following): activities of rival firms; consumer preferences; economic activity.
. Possible answers (two of the following):
   Higher prices can make people think goods are worth more.
   Promotions can inform customers about the new features of a new version of a product to raise excitement.
   Products can be updated regularly so that customers do not lose interest in them.
   Place can make it easier for customers to access products by selecting a wider range of distribution channels.
. Possible answer (one of the following):
   controls on the quality of goods;
   controls on the accuracy of messages in adverts.

The opportunities and problems of entering new foreign markets: Quick test (page 54)

. In order to extend the product lifecycle of their goods/services;
   in order to increase profits made;
   in order to meet the needs of new customers.
. The shared values and norms of people in a specific area.
. Possible answer: it might inform the way the working day is organised; for example, it might be traditional to have a break in the middle of the day for workers to sleep in countries with a hot climate. It might lead to tasks being designed to accommodate the way people prefer to work.
   When two companies invest in a business opportunity together.
. So that the risk of entering the market is minimised;
   so that a company with better local knowledge can build awareness of the brand in the foreign market.

Exam-style practice questions (pages 55–56)

a) Customer needs are the things that a person requires [1] to have a positive experience from a business [1]. **[2 marks]**
b) Customers are people who buy products [1] while consumers are people who use products [1]. **[2 marks]**
c) Niche markets can be more profitable [1] because there are often fewer competitors [1] and higher prices can be charged [1] because customers are likely to be less price sensitive [1]. **[4 marks]**
d) The market for train travel might change because of new technology [1] such as a better engine for trains [1] that is more fuel-efficient [1].

Another reason that the market might change is if the products that customers demand change [1] such as a reduction in the number of people travelling to work by train [1] or more people choosing to drive to their leisure destinations [1]. **[6 marks]**
e) Demographic segmenation is splitting the market up according to people's incomes [1]; this might allow Haliva to target more affluent customers [1] with more expensive tickets [1]; on the other hand, behavioural segmentation is likely to be more appropriate [1] because it allows the company to target people according to whether they are travelling for work or leisure [1] and might give some insights into extra services that would entice them such as wifi on trains [1]. **[6 marks]**

2. a) Method one: a survey [1] which would involve sending a questionnaire to a sample of potential customers [1]. Method two: a focus group [1] which would involve organising a conversation with a group of consumers [1]. Method three: observation [1], watching people using or shopping for a specific product or service [1]. Method four: foot-count [1], seeing how many people visit a certain place at different times [1]. **[8 marks]**
b) Large samples would make research more accurate [1] because they would reduce the chance of data being skewed [1] by outliers [1] such as cases of anomalous customer behaviour [1].
   Representative samples would give a clear picture of what the target market want [1] because they are based on the type of people in the target market [1].
   Recent research is more likely to reflect the latest trends [1] and so will give a more accurate picture because it is less likely to be out-of-date [1] when analysing it [1].
   Overall, the most important factor is representative samples because data should give information about actual customers [1] and not just a group of people whose opinions might differ [1] and therefore give invalid data [1]. **[12 marks]**
c) One implication of a product in the growth stage is that it will cost a lot of money to promote it [1] because it is still new and so customers will need to know about it [1] and so there might need to be expensive mass media advertising campaigns [1] such as television advertising to create as much awareness as possible [1].
   Another implication is that there will be a lot of competition [1] because other firms will see the product becoming successful [1] and will start to launch their own versions of it [1] increasing the chances of customers buying a different product [1]. **[8 marks]**
d) Loyal customers are likely to be less price-sensitive [1] because they have a preference for one product over any competing product [1] because they would rather buy it than anything else [1].
   If there is a lack of competition then customers may not have the option to buy an alternative product [1] meaning that no matter how high the premium price is [1] they would still have to buy it if that is what they are looking for [1].
   Price-insensitive customers buy based on factors other than the price of goods [1] which means that they are not likely to be concerned by a high price point [1] as they are mainly interested in the brand and the value that they think it represents [1].
   Overall, the most important factor is likely to be customer loyalty [1] because that creates price insensitivity [1] and will lead to customers paying as much money as they can afford because they are likely to strongly desire the product [1]. **[12 marks]**

e) Factor one: necessity **[1]**: if people have to buy something [for example, petrol] then they are likely to pay for it even when it's expensive **[1]**.
Factor two: time **[1]**: in the short term, people might not be able to shop around for alternatives **[1]**.
Factor three: disposable income **[1]**: the more of this customers have, the less sensitive they are likely to be to price **[1]**.
Factor four: the number of substitutes **[1]**: if there is nothing that can replace the product then demand will be less price elastic **[1]**. **[8 marks]**

f) Selling more tickets via box offices will have a higher profit margin **[1]** because the tickets will be sold direct to customers **[1]** and so revenues will not have to be shared with other firms **[1]**; however, there will be overheads involved in running box offices **[1]** such as the cost of rent and electricity **[1]** which will reduce the profits made **[1]** whereas selling more tickets through agents might be good because these companies will specialise in selling tickets **[1]** and so will have more expertise in marketing and promotion for these goods **[1]** and so therefore they might be able to sell much larger quantities **[1]**. But overall the company should stick to selling the tickets via their box offices because although they will have overheads to pay, these fixed costs **[1]** can be split over a larger number of sales **[1]** increasing the contribution earned on each ticket **[1]**. **[12 marks]**

Chapter 4 Operations management

The meaning of production: Quick test (page 58)
1. Production is what is made while productivity is how much of something is made in a given period of time.
2. Efficiency is how well resources such as machinery, people and money, are used.
3. Just in time stock control, Kaizen.
4. Waste is eliminated, therefore reducing costs. This should lead to higher profits and also to higher quality products as the business continuously improves what it makes and empowers workers to find ways to do their jobs better.

The main methods of production: Quick test (page 60)
1. Job; batch; flow.
2. Possible answers: the process can be partially automated. It allows flexibility to meet varied customer needs.
3. Possible answers: there are high capital costs for setting up this method. Products are all homogenous – there is no scope to adapt them to meet specific customer needs.
4. Possible answers: CAD systems allow prototypes and finished designs to be completed more quickly. CAM systems allow smaller quantities of goods to be produced more cost-effectively. Additive manufacturing allows rapid prototyping of new ideas. CADCAM systems make production functions more adaptable.

Scale of production – economies and diseconomies of scale: Quick test (page 62)
1. Making large numbers of identical products in a continuous flow.
2. Orders can be customised according to the needs of specific customers/groups. Goods are made in larger quantities, which may give scope for some economies of scale.
3. The reduction of the average cost per unit as output increases.
4. Bulk-buying – getting discounts for ordering more goods; technical economies – lowering costs by investing in machinery.
5. If a business grows too big, it might be hard to co-ordinate activities, leading to increasing costs and thereby reducing the profitability of the business.

Identify and classify costs: Quick test (page 63)
1. $5 × 200 units = $1000.
2. $1000 + $800 = $1800.
3. $1800 ÷ 200 = $9.

Break-even analysis: Quick test (page 65)
1. The difference between break-even output and the predicted number of goods sold.
2. 150 units
3. 250 units
4. (250 units – 150 units =) 100 units
5. $1000
6. $2000 ÷ 150 units = $13.33
7.

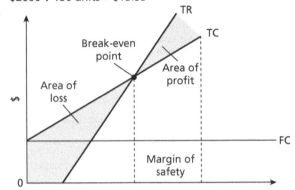

8. The analysis does not take into account external factors, for example, inflation might cause costs to rise, increasing the break-even point. The analysis does not guarantee that the firm will reach the break-even level of output.

Why quality is important and how quality production might be achieved: Quick test (page 66)
1. Higher quality goods will be more effective in meeting customer needs. Higher quality will mean less wastage and thus lower costs.
2. Quality control inspects goods at the end of the production process; it makes quality 'someone else's problem'. Quality assurance empowers all workers to take responsibility for the quality of what is produced.

The main factors influencing the location and relocation decisions of a business: Quick test (page 68)
1. Transport links; availability of skilled workers; availability of raw materials.
2. Possible answers: transport links – so that customers can get to the business; proximity to suppliers – so that the business can respond to sudden changes in demand; availability of staff – so that customers always have the right level of service.
3. The culture of the country – whether the product/service is acceptable there; language barriers – communication with staff/customers; laws and regulations – how will they affect the activities of a firm?

Exam-style practice questions (pages 69–70)
1. a) Productivity is the amount of work that is completed **[1]** during a given period of time **[1]**. **[2 marks]**
   b) Lean management is a range of techniques designed to reduce waste **[1]** of business resources such as raw materials, money and time **[1]**. **[2 marks]**
   c) Job production allows small numbers of goods to be produced so there is less waste **[1]** as they are only making items that customers are likely to want **[1]** which allows the business to tailor products to customer requirements **[1]** increasing customer satisfaction **[1]**. **[4 marks]**
   d) Purchasing economies of scale **[1]** are gained when a firm orders large quantities of stock **[1]** leading to suppliers giving them a discounted price per unit **[1]**. Managerial economies of scale **[1]** come from hiring staff with specialist skills **[1]** such as operations managers **[1]**. **[6 marks]**

e) Break-even analysis tells a business how many items must be sold to cover fixed and variable costs [1] which helps produce appropriate production schedules [1] but it does not protect a firm from changes in the external environment [1] such as an unexpected recession [1]; overall, break-even analysis helps a business to make plans that allow them to be profitable [1] but must review them as the business environment changes [1].
[6 marks]

2. a) Benefit one: it allows the business to promote special offer prices [1] which would move the break-even point further to the right [1].
Benefit two: it allows the business to cope with falls in demand [1] such as when a recession occurs [1].
Benefit three: it allows a business to cope with increases in costs [1], for example, if raw materials become more expensive [1].
Benefit four: it allows a margin of error if the break-even point has been calculated incorrectly [1], for example, by using inaccurate data to create it [1].

b) If quality is the responsibility of every worker, then they will always check the products that they handle [1]. Allowing defects to be identified sooner [1] and potentially corrected more easily [1].
Constant checks on products mean that there is less chance of mistakes being missed [1] which would prevent poor quality goods being sold to the public [1] and reduce the number of items returned [1].
If all staff know quality standards then anyone can spot problems [1] which means that people can find errors even if it is not a part of the job that they normally do [1] reducing the risk of errors being missed [1]. Overall, the most important factor is the knowledge of the standards because without this staff couldn't check products [1] and wouldn't be able to find errors [1] or might make inconsistent decisions [1]. **[12 marks]**

c) Reason one: it means products stand out from those of competitors [1] by giving them a unique characteristic [1]. Reason two: it improves customer satisfaction [1] increasing the chance of repeat purchases [1]. Reason three: it increases the value for money offered by the products [1] making people happier to pay for them [1]. Reason four: it improves the reputation of the business [1] making customers happier to shop there [1].
[8 marks]

d) Being near transport links means that the business can get orders to customers quicker [1] because they are able to move vans and lorries in and out of their factory faster [1] which allows them to respond more effectively [1] to changes in demand from customers [1]; on the other hand, being close to skilled workers means that they are more likely to be able to hire the right people to make their products [1] leading to fewer production errors [1] and therefore a better product overall [1].
Modern technology such as route-planning software means that being close to roads is less important [1] because the computer programs can find the best way [1] to make deliveries on time [1] but it's hard to find skilled workers [1] so it would be better to be close to skilled staff [1]. **[12 marks]**

Chapter 5 Financial information and decisions

Business finance: needs and sources: Quick test (page 72)
A new business will need to invest heavily in items such as machinery, staff recruitment and training, and stock, and will need to advertise to make customers aware of its opening. Having enough money to do these things well is of great importance.
2. If a business wants to expand rapidly, it might be necessary to add extra capacity, for example, hire more staff and buy more machinery, and this will require investment. Even when a business grows slowly, there will be limits on its capacity that will need to be addressed, for example, hiring extra staff to operate machinery overnight or at weekends.
3. Cash that is available from day to day to pay the costs of running the business.
4. Short-term sources of finance tend to be more expensive and should only be used to address shortfall in working capital so that the business can keep its operations running from day to day. Long-term sources of finance are cheaper and are more appropriate for larger investments such as expansion.

The importance of cash and of cashflow forecasting: Quick test (page 73)
1. In order to predict periods of time when the business might be short of cash so that they can make appropriate plans, such as organising credit or rescheduling expenditure.
2. Net cashflow = cash inflows – cash outflows
3. $900

Cashflow forecasting: Quick test (page 75)
1. March
2. By reducing the amount of money spent in February and/or March to ensure that it is less than the inflows in those months. Alternatively, by increasing inflows in February and/or March.
3. February and March
4. April.

Income statements – what profit is and why it is important: Quick test (page 77)
1. Cash is money that the business has available to spend from day to day. This can come from sources such as revenue or from credit sources such as an overdraft. Profit is money that belongs to the business. It is what is left when costs are deducted from revenues.
2. Profits are important because the owners of a business expect profits as a reward for the risk that they took in investing in the business. Profits are also important because retained profits can be used to invest in the future growth of the business, and unlike loan capital this does not have to be paid back.
3. Revenue increased by $3000 from 2017 to 2018.
4. Cost of sales is $1000 lower in 2018 despite the business having more sales. This suggests that it is doing a better job of managing its variable costs.
5. 2017 – the costs were $1000 lower.
6. 2017

The main elements of a statement of financial position: Quick test (page 79)
1. To show the value of a business at a given point in time.
2. Cash; stock.
3. Current assets can be turned to cash in less than a year, while non-current assets can only be turned into cash in a year or more.
4. Current liabilities must be paid off within a year, while long-term liabilities can be paid off in a period of time greater than a year.
5. Current assets – current liabilities = –$29 000
6. $46 000
7. $21 000
8. $8000

The concept and importance of profitability: Quick test (page 80)
1. Profit is money that you have left after costs have been paid. Profitability is how efficiently you are managing costs.
2. The difference between the selling price of an item and the cost of producing it.

3. Liquidity refers to how much cash a business has available. It is important because a business that is illiquid will not be able to pay its bills and may become insolvent.

Calculating and analysing profitability ratios and liquidity ratios: Quick test (page 82)

1. If profit margins are small, this might mean that a business cannot afford to cut prices. If profit margins are large, this may mean that costs are being controlled very well or that too little money is being spent on raw materials, compromising quality.
2. ROCE indicates how much return is made on the money being invested in a business.
3. The acid test ratio shows a business whether it can settle its debts without selling any stock.

Why and how accounts are used: Quick test (page 83)

1. Investors would want to know how well a business is performing so they know how much risk they are taking. Bankers would want to know if the business is able to pay its debts before lending it more money or agreeing an overdraft.
2. Ratio analysis is a snapshot of performance at a point in time. It tells you about past performance but does not guarantee that the business will continue to perform that way in the future.

Exam-style practice questions (pages 84–85)

1. a) Short term finance is when small sums of money are borrowed [1] for periods of time such as a week or a month [1]. **[2 marks]**
   b) Working capital is the cash that a business uses from day to day [1] in order to keep paying its operating costs [1]. **[2 marks]**
   c) A cashflow forecast will identify periods of time when there is sufficient cash to make a large purchase [1] and will allow managers to plan to borrow cash if they will not have enough cash [1]; it will be possible to test the impact of a large purchase on working capital [1] to make sure that the business doesn't run out of money [1]. **[4 marks]**
   d) An overdraft is an expensive source of credit [1] because it charges a high interest rate [1] on a daily basis [1]. An overdraft is also designed for smaller sums of money [1] meaning that if a large amount of cash is needed [1] it might not have a high enough limit to allow managers access to the funds they need [1]. **[6 marks]**
   e) 2017
      Gross profit = $64 000 – $60 000 = $4000 [1]
      Net profit = $4000 – $9000 = – $5000 [1]

      2018
      Gross profit = $95 000 – $45 000 = $50 000 [1]
      Net profit = $50 000 – $12 000 = $38 000 [1]

      Overall, the business has $38 000 profit from 2018 and this has grown significantly since 2017 [1], an increase of $43 000 which suggests that retained profit is now a realistic source of finance [1]. **[6 marks]**
2. a) Statement of financial position shows the assets and liabilities [1] of a business at a given point in time [1]. **[2 marks]**
   b) A current asset is something that can be turned into cash in less than one year [1] such as stock [1]. **[2 marks]**
   c) Current assets / current liabilities = current ratio [1]
      2017: 53/47 = 1.13 [1]
      2018: 56/49 = 1.14 [1]

      There has been no significant change in the ratio and the business can still pay all of its current liabilities using its current assets [1]. **[4 marks]**

   d) The acid test is when inventories are deducted from current assets [1] in order to calculate whether a firm can pay its current liabilities [1] which means they can see if debts can be paid without selling stock [1]. Another advantage is that the ratio takes away any distortions caused to liquidity [1] by a seasonal business holding large amounts of stock, for example, toy shops at Christmas [1], giving a more accurate picture of liquidity [1]. **[6 marks]**
   e) Holding less stock would be beneficial because holding stock ties up cash [1] that might be better spent on paying day-to-day bills [1] and this would improve the financial efficiency of the business [1]. However, reducing the amount of time that customers are given to pay may be a better idea because this would increase the amount of cash coming into the business each month [1] and would mean that the business would be less likely to need to use short-term finance such as trade credit/overdrafts [1] which might have expensive interest rates [1]. **[6 marks]**

Chapter 6 External influences on business activity

Business cycle: Quick test (page 88)

1. GDP growth, low inflation, low unemployment.
2. Gross domestic product – it is a measure of national income.
3. To reduce the amount of money they spend on unemployment benefit; to improve GDP – more people earning money will mean more spending on goods and services, leading to higher national income.
4. Governments want to ensure that businesses trying to export have access to markets while at the same time they want to make sure that citizens have access to a range of goods and services from abroad.
5. The rise in price levels over time.
6. Inflation increases the costs to a business as prices rise, but it also increases the prices that a business can charge. Inflation will potentially increase wage bills because staff will demand higher salaries.
7. To fund investment in infrastructure; to provide essential services like health and education; to fund benefits.
8. Value added tax (VAT); income tax; corporation tax.
9. Tax increases will increase costs to a business. They will lead to lower consumer spending because more of consumers' income has to be paid to the government.
10. Consumers will save more of their income and will borrow less money from banks.

Environmental and ethical Issues: Quick test (page 90)

1. Child labour; pollution; exploitation of developing countries; deforestation; childhood obesity.
2. Global warming; air pollution.
3. Managers have a legal obligation to make the highest possible profit for the owners of a business. Therefore, unless there is a law stating that they must use production methods which cause less pollution, they will be obliged to continue with the cheapest option.

The importance of globalisation: Quick test (page 92)

1. The increasing interconnectedness of the world, which allows trade between an increasing range of countries.
2. Possible answers: Walmart; McDonald's; Coca-Cola.
3. A greater choice of goods and services; lower prices due to lower costs from the economies of scale gained from the global scale of operation.

4. Global firms will pay taxes in whichever country has the lowest rates. Global firms may move jobs offshore.

Business and the international economy:

Quick test (page 94)
1. The price of one currency in terms of another.
2. The cost of buying goods from abroad (imports) decreases and the cost of goods sold overseas (exports) goes up.
3. Exporters will have a higher profit margin because the price of their goods will increase abroad. However, they may have less revenue if their goods have price elastic demand.

Exam-style practice questions (pages 95–96)
1. a) Business cycle is the pattern of rising and falling GDP in an economy [1] as it moves from recession to boom [1].
   [2 marks]
   b) Inflation is the tendency for prices to rise over time [1] measured by the change in value of a basket of goods [1]. **[2 marks]**
   c) The government might use tax cuts [1] to make people feel wealthier and therefore spend more money [1] or they might increase government spending on infrastructure such as roads [1] to stimulate growth by putting money in the hands of firms [1]. **[4 marks]**
   d) The businesses might choose to pass the tax increase on to customers [1] which would increase the prices that they pay [1] and therefore will reduce demand if customers are price-sensitive [1].
   Alternatively, the firm might choose to bear the cost of the tax increase itself [1] increasing its costs of sales [1] and leading to lower profits [1]. **[6 marks]**
   e) People who are saving money will receive a greater return on their investment [1] increasing the amount of money they earn each month [1] whereas the cost of borrowing money [1] will be higher each month [1] and since borrowers will have no choice but to make their repayments each month [1] the greatest impact will be on them, especially if they have borrowed large amounts of money [1]. **[6 marks]**
2. a) Benefit one: it reduces the impact of climate change [1] as firms will operate in a more environmentally friendly way [1].
   Benefit two: it improves quality of life for communities [1] by providing employment opportunities [1].
   Benefit three: economic growth is increased [1] leading to higher tax revenues for governments [1].
   Benefit four: new technologies are introduced into developing economies [1] leading to higher potential growth in the future [1]. **[8 marks]**

   b) Investment in technology will improve the environmental performance of the business [1] but the cost of the investment will lower profits [1] as will ongoing maintenance costs [1].
   Strict rules and procedures might mean that certain orders cannot be taken [1], for example, it might not be possible to produce a batch of chemicals quickly [1] because the rules and procedures include time-consuming precautions [1].
   High levels of training and education for staff will be expensive [1] and although it will improve the quality of the work that is carried out [1] it might also lead to staff becoming more attractive to competitors leading to higher staff turnover [1].
   Overall, the greatest conflict is between the profits of the business and the training of staff because the firm has an incentive not to train staff [1] in case they move on to a competing firm using the training [1] which is bad for the workers and the environment [1]. **[12 marks]**
   c) Benefit one: it increases the quality of life for citizens of the countries involved [1] because they will have access to a wider range of goods and services [1].
   Benefit two: it improves economic efficiency [1] as countries can concentrate on production where they have a relative advantage [1].
   Benefit three: it increases competition in markets [1] leading to reductions in the power of firms and thus lower prices [1].
   Benefit four: it allows firms to operate across multiple markets [1] increasing the size of the economies of scale they can access [1]. **[8 marks]**
   d) Drawing water from rivers will mean less water is available for farmers and citizens [1] which will increase their costs of business/living [1] even though they do not benefit from the activities of Clean Corporation [1].
   High rates of cancer might be related to the waste chemicals from the factory [1] polluting the water, air or soil near the factory [1] whether people work there or not [1].
   Low wages and long hours for employees will reduce their quality of life and that of their families [1], for example, it might put more pressure on their partners to raise their children [1] while the firm makes large profits on the goods that they produce [1].
   The most significant factor is likely to be the high rates of cancer as this will lead to significant financial hardship for the families of the cancer patients [1] while the firm bears none of the costs associated [1] unless the country has laws that lead to Clean Corporation being fined [1]. **[12 marks]**

Glossary

Adding value – The process of transforming raw materials into finished goods and consequently increasing the amount of money that a customer is willing to pay for them.

Advertising – Paying for space in media channels such as on TV or in newspapers.

Affluent consumers – People with a higher income and/or large disposable income.

Annual general meeting (AGM) – A meeting between the directors of a limited company and its shareholders which must be held at least once a year.

Appreciation – An increase in the value of a currency.

Autocratic – A leadership style where workers are given orders and expected to comply with them.

Automation – When jobs previously completed by workers are now fully or partially completed by machinery.

Average costs – Total costs divided by total output.

Balance of trade – The difference between the monetary value of a country's exports and imports over a certain period.

Batch production – Making a small quantity of identical products.

Benchmarking – The process of comparing the performance of one firm with that of another.

Benefits – Social security payments used as a 'safety net' to prevent extreme poverty.

Boom – When an economy is performing well and GDP is high

and/or rising, leading to higher living standards.

Brand image – How a brand is perceived by customers and by the general public.

Branding – The use of elements such as a name, symbol and/or logo to distinguish your product/business from those of other firms.

Break-even – The point at which total revenue and total costs are equal.

Bricks and mortar – A traditional business with physical premises (for example, a shop) but no online presence.

Budget – A target for spending on a specific business activity.

Business cycle – The stages that an economy goes through, from boom to bust.

Business plan – A document which outlines the intended activities of a new or existing business.

CADCAM – Computer Aided Design, Computer Aided Manufacture. The use of specialist software and tools to produce prototypes and finished goods.

Capability – The extent to which an employee is able to do their job.

Capital expenditure – Making long-term investments, for example, the purchase of new machinery.

Cash – Liquid finance that can be accessed imediately.

Cashflow – The money which "flows" in and out of a business.

Chain of command – The distance between the person at the top of an organisation and the staff at the bottom of the hierarchy. The series of steps that an instruction has to go through to reach its intended recipient.

Collective bargaining – When a trade union negotiates on behalf of all of the employees in a firm.

Communication – The transmission of a message from one party to another.

Communication barriers – Things which prevent effective communication from taking place.

Competition – One or more businesses which are aiming to lure customers away from your products to theirs.

Competitive – The extent to which a business is able to effectively compete against other firms in the same market.

Competitive pricing – When goods or services are sold for a price that is around the same as those set by competitors.

Conduct – The behaviour of an employee, both on and off the job.

Conglomerate – A group of businesses operating in different markets which sell differing products but share some back office functions such as finance and HR.

Consumer – Someone who uses product or service.

Contract – A legal agreement between two parties, for example, a business and its customers, or a business and its employees.

Correlation – When there is a relationship between two different factors - that changes in one lead to changes in the other.

Cost-plus pricing – When a desired profit margin is added to the cost of producing goods or services.

Crowdsourcing – When a product is offered for sale in advance of its launch so customers can commit to buying it, thereby funding the cost of production.

Culture – The collected behaviours of people in a specific business or country.

Customer – Someone who buys a product or service.

Customer loyalty – The extent to which customers return to a business to make repeat purchases.

Customer needs – The things that are required by a customer in order to have a satisfactory experience when using a business.

Customer relationships – When a business knows and understands the needs of customers in order to satisfy their needs on an ongoing basis.

Customer service – The process of identifying and meeting the needs of customers.

Debt – Money owed to financial institutions such as banks.

Deed of partnership – A document which outlines the rights and responsibilities of each of the owners of a partnership business.

Delegation – When a senior member of staff gives a colleague the authority to complete a task.

Demand – The number of goods or services that customers are willing to buy at a given price.

Democratic – A leadership style where the views and opinions of workers are considered when making decisions.

Depreciation – A fall in the value of something.

Discrimination – Treating an individual or group of employees differently to other employees.

Diseconomies of scale – The tendency for average unit costs to rise when a business grows too large.

Distribution channel – The route that a business uses to get its products onto the market.

Domestic industry – Business in your home country.

Early adopters – A group of potential customers that like to buy the most up-to-date versions of products and new technologies.

E-commerce – The buying and selling of goods and services online.

Economies of scale – The tendency for average unit costs to decrease as a business grows.

Economy – A system for exchanging goods and services for money in order to meet the needs of its participants.

Efficiency – The use of the lowest possible amounts of inputs (for example, labour, machinery, raw materials) to produce the greatest possible quantity of goods and services.

Elastic demand – The level of demand will change proportionately more than a change in price.

Employment tribunal – An independent panel which can make judgements about the legality of business decisions about the employment of staff.

Enterprise – Can either be used as another term for business, or can be used to describe the demonstration of entrepreneurial characteristics by an individual or company.

Entrepreneurship – When an individual or group of people take risks in order to establish and run a business.

Equity – Money invested in a firm, for example, by shareholders.

Ethics – The extent to which a business complies with legal and moral obligations.

Exchange rate – The price of one currency in terms of another.

Extension strategy – Marketing activity designed to extend the product lifecycle of existing goods and services.

Externalities – Costs or benefits affecting those not directly involved in business transactions.

External Recruitment – Appointing a person from outside an organisation to a job role.

Fixed costs – Costs which do not change in response to a change in the number of customers served or products produced.

Flow production – Continuously making large quantities of identical products.

Franchise – An agreement to allow a business or an entrepreneur to use the intellectual property of an established firm.

Franchisee – A person buying the rights to a franchise.

Franchisor – A firm selling the rights to a franchise agreement.

Full employment – When everyone in a country who wants a job is able to get one.

GDP (Gross Domestic Product) – A way of measuring national income.

Globalisation – The extent to which economic activity in different countries increasingly depend on one another.

Hygiene factors – According to Herzberg, these factors will not cause motivation on their own, but their absence from the workplace will cause demotivation.

Import tariff – A tax charged on goods imported into a country.

Income statement – A financial document showing how much money a business has earned, how much it has spent and how much profit/loss it has made in a given period of time.

Industrial action – When workers refuse to complete some or all of their work as a protest against problems with their working conditions or treatment by managers.

Inelastic demand – The level of demand will change proportionately less than changes in price.

Inflation – The tendency for the price of goods and services to rise over time, reducing the value of money.

Infrastructure – Roads, railways, electricity production and other important services which facilitate economic activity.

Intermediary – A stage in a distribution channel between the manufacturer and the customer.

Internal recruitment – Appointing an existing member of staff to a new role.

Inventories – The stock held by a business. Can be a combination of finished goods and unfinished goods.

Job description – A document which outlines the role, responsibilities and tasks to be carried out by a specific worker or group of employees.

Job production – Making a product or delivering a service as a 'one-off'.

Job role – The tasks that a specific employee is expected to carry out and the responsibilites they are expected to take on.

Joint venture – When two businesses collaborate on a project such as launching a new product into a new market, sharing costs and risks.

Just In Time (JIT) – When a business only holds enough stock to last until its next delivery arrives.

Kaizen – A Japanese management philosophy based on making continual improvements to business processes.

Knowledge economy – When a country's economy relies primarily on high added-value service jobs such as banking and computer programming.

Laissez-faire – A leadership style where workers are given freedom to carry out their job in the way that they see fit.

Lead time – The time between placing an order and receiving the goods or services ordered.

Lean production – The elimination of waste from business processes.

Licensing – When a business allows another firm to use its intellectual property in exchange for a fee.

Limited company – A type of incorporated business which is owned by shareholders.

Limited liability – When shareholders only lose the money that they have invested in a business if it fails.

Liquidity – The amount of assets belonging to a business that are convertible to cash in the short term.

Margin of safety – The gap between the number of products sold by a business and the number of products required to break even.

Marketing mix – A framework for planning marketing activity, based around the four Ps: Product, Price, Place and Promotion.

Market orientation – When a business focuses on producing goods and services that meet the needs and wants of customers.

Market segmentation – When a group of customers or consumer are divided up into groups which have similar needs to allow businesses to more accurately target people who are likely to want specific products or services

Mass market – A larger market with a large number of customers with relatively similar needs and wants.

Merger – When two firms join together to form a new, larger organsiation.

Microfinance – Small loans often used to stimulate business activity in developing countries.

Mixed economy – When an economy comprises a mixture of public and private sector businesses.

Motivation – The state of mind when an individual or group wants to do something.

Motivators – According to Herzberg, these are things that will lead to an individual becoming motivated to do something.

Multinational company (MNC) – A business which operates in multiple countries.

Negative externality – When business activity has a negative effect on individuals and groups that are not directly involved in their transactions.

Niche market – A smaller group of customers with very specific needs and wants.

Objectives – The targets or goals set by a business in order to achieve its overall aims.

Off-the-job training – When an employee is sent to an external provider such as a college or university for training.

On-the-job training – Training activity undertaken alongside the normal work of a member of staff.

Opportunity cost – The cost of choosing one option stated in terms of the option that you choose to forgo.

Overdraft – A short-term source of finance which allows businesses to borrow money flexibly.

Partnership – When a business is owned by two or more people.

Penetration pricing – When a product is launched with a low price with the aim of encouraging people to try it.

Person specification – A document which outlines the skills, attributes and experience that an applicant for a specific job role should have.

Positive externality – When business activity has a positive effect on individuals and groups that are not directly involved in their transactions.

Price elasticity – The extent to which demand for a product is responsive to a change in the price of that product.

Price skimming – When a high price is set when a product is launched to take advantage of customers willing to pay more for something new.

Primary industry – Businesses that extract raw materials from the ground or the sea.

Primary research – New research which has been gathered for a specific purpose.

Private sector business – When firms are owned by private individuals or other firms.

Production – When a business makes goods or services.

Productivity – The quantity of goods or services that can be produced in a specific period of time using a given quantity of raw materials and equipment.

Product lifecycle – The stages that a product goes through from its launch until its withdrawal from the market.

Product orientation – When a business focuses on the development of a sophisticated product, without considering the things that customers say they want and need.

Profit – The difference between revenue and costs.

Profitability – The extent to which a business is able to control costs and maximise revenues.

Profit margin – The difference between the cost of producing goods or services and their selling price.

Promotion – When a business communicates with its customers.

Promotional pricing – When special offers such as a discount or a multibuy offer are used to encourage customers to purchase items.

Protectionism – When government policy is designed to protect domestic businesses at the expense of foreign companies.

Public sector business – When firms are owned by government.

Quality – The standards achieved in the production of goods and services.

Quality assurance – When products are continually checked throughout the process of production.

Quality control – When a product is checked for errors at the end of the production process.

Quota – A limit on the number of goods that can be imported into a country.

Ration – When the quantity of goods or services that a person is able to buy is limited. This could be by a government or by the functioning of the market mechanism.

Raw materials – Components, parts and ingredients that a business uses to produce goods and services.

Recession – Two or more consecutive quarters of negative GDP growth, leading to lower living standards.

Redundancy – When a specific job role is no longer needed by a business.

Responsibilities – Tasks or targets that an employee has to complete to a given standard.

Retailer – A business which sells goods or services directly to customers.

Revenue expenditure – The day-to-day costs of running a business.

Sales promotion – The use of promotional pricing to stimulate the purchase of goods.

Sampling – The process of selecting a group which can represent the whole population when carrying out research.

Scarcity – In a world of unlimited wants, we only have a limited quantity of resources to produce goods and services.

Secondary industry – Businesses that process raw materials and produce goods.

Secondary research – Existing research which has already been published.

Shortlist – A selection of applicants for a job who are considered worth inviting for an interview.

Social enterprise – A business organisation which has been established to pursue a social purpose such as alleviating poverty.

Sole trader – When a business is owned by a single individual.

Span of control – The number of staff that a manager or supervisor is expected to monitor and control.

Specialisation – Focusing on the production of a single specific good or service.

Stakeholder – Anyone with an interest in or who is affected by the activities of a business.

Statement of financial position – A financial document showing the assets and liabilities that fund a business.

Subsidies – Payments by governments to businesses to encourage the production of particular goods or services.

Suppliers – Businesses which provide raw materials or services to other businesses.

Takeover – When one business purchases another business and absorbs it, creating a single, larger firm.

Taxes – Payments to government by citizens and by businesses. Usually a fixed percentage of the cost of goods purchased or of income.

Tertiary industry – Businesses that provide a service, either to other firms or to consumers.

Total costs – The sum of fixed costs and variable costs.

Trade payables – The money owed to a supplier for goods or services provided if they are bought on credit.

Trade union – A group which represents the rights of workers and negotiates on their behalf.

Training – Developing the skills and providing experience of completing tasks for employees.

Transactional website – A website that allows customers to pay for goods and services online.

Unincorporated business – A business such as a sole trader or partnership that has no separate legal identity from its owner.

Unlimited liability – When the personal assets of a business owner can be taken to settle debts.

Variable costs – The cost of producing each of the goods or services sold by a firm.

Voluntary redundancy – When employees choose to be made redundant, normally in exchange for a more generous financial settlement – a tactic sometimes employed when a company is downsizing or restructuring.

Wholesaler – A business which buys products in bulk from manufacturers and then sells smaller quantities on to retailers.

Working capital – The cash used to run a business from day to day.